THE RELEVANCE OF JESUS' *Own Gospel*

THE VIEWS OF A PHYSICS TEACHER

The Relevance of Jesus' Own Gospel: The Views of a Physics Teacher

Published in the United States of America

Library of Congress Control Number: 2024904561
ISBN Paperback: 979-8-89091-417-0
ISBN eBook: 979-8-89091-418-7

ReadersMagnet, LLC
10620 Treena Street, Suite 230 | San Diego, California, 92131 USA
1. 619. 354. 2643 | www. readersmagnet.com

Cover design by Tifanny Curaza
Interior design by Daniel Lopez

THE RELEVANCE OF JESUS' *Own Gospel*

THE VIEWS OF A PHYSICS TEACHER

ALLEN C. DOTSON

ReadersMagnet, LLC

Dedicated to you, the reader

Contents

PREFACE

Before you decide to read from this book, I should give you an idea of what it concerns. For me, the relevance of Jesus' *gospel*—his "good news"—depends on two things: the proposition that God had a uniquely close relationship with Jesus, thereby making Jesus' ministry relevant to *his* times, and the proposition that Jesus' ministry carries a message relevant to *our* times. Corresponding to those two propositions, my goal in the book is to present as strong a case as I can in support of two beliefs that I hold: (1) that God, pictured much as Jesus described God in his teachings, was directly responsible for some post-crucifixion appearances of Jesus; and (2) that in so acting, God validated that part of the message Jesus taught, through both words and deeds, which is most relevant to later generations, including those of today's world.

In Chapters 1 through 4, I explain how I, a physics professor by trade, see strong evidence for the first of those beliefs provided by the nature of science and some pretty unassailable claims of historical fact. Religion is much more a matter of the heart than of the mind, and the primary basis of my Christian faith is what I believe to be true about matters that have no direct support from objective facts. The depth of my convictions, however, can often use some indirect support of a more objective nature, and that is what I hope to explain clearly in the first four chapters of this book.

The remainder of the book deals with the relevance of Jesus' message for our times, as I understand that message to be. This part is just the opinion of one person—and a non-theologian, at that. It is a well-known fact that in studying the Bible, people tend to interpret whatever passages they encounter from whatever viewpoint they already have. I certainly cannot claim to be exempt from that tendency. My perspective on Jesus' basic message is mostly woven together from the writings of several New Testament scholars and theologians, to whom I will often refer.

As I'll explain at the beginning of Chapter 2, this book does not discuss several key doctrines of traditional Christianity. My focus is on the ministry of Jesus in this world in the first century of the Christian Era (CE), as scholars can best reconstruct it. I try to keep to the purpose I indicated: to defend belief in a God who loves everybody with unbounded love, and who showed that love by causing, in some way and in some form, post-crucifixion appearances of Jesus, "God's Anointed." This belief carries an important message beyond Christianity as it is traditionally conceived, and I would hope that my defense of it will be of some interest to non-Christians of all sorts.

For centuries, and especially since the publication of Freud's *The Future of an Illusion*, some scientists have attempted to explain away not just Christianity but all religions as solely products of the human mind. This book responds in part to that view, which I view as an illusion. Many other persons in scientific or science-related careers have written books detailing solid reasons in support of their religious beliefs. Nevertheless, some people, who may or may not work in science themselves but admire the great advances that science has made in modern times, wonder how scientists could believe in a God who cares about humanity. My own reasons for belief are not revolutionary or even new, but some particular facts that speak strongly to me may not have received the attention that I feel they deserve, and so I am adding my thoughts as well. First, I will focus on science in relation to religion. Then I will turn to first-century history, as the majority of historians seem to understand it. And finally, I will rely on several authorities in the interpretation of Jesus' ministry to discuss my own understanding of the chief message of that ministry and how it relates to our own times.

PART 1:

The Basics

1

About Science

Prior to beginning the development of my arguments for the two specific beliefs outlined in the preface, I want to address some broader issues about belief in God. In this age, when scientific evidence is viewed as objective, quantitative, and capable of being tested and retested, questions arise about whether faith in God is a reasonable option for educated people. For some, these questions seem difficult enough to preclude any sort of serious interest in faith in a loving, powerful God. In this book I will address three such questions in descending order of their scope:

1. Religious beliefs cannot be supported by hard experimental evidence in the way that scientific beliefs can. A naturally arising question is whether religious experience, as subjective and personal as

most of it is, can reliably provide any insights at all about the nature of reality. I address this question here in Chapter 1.

2. The question that often arises is whether God could play any significant role in the events of this world, which seems to be governed by true, unbreakable laws of nature, toward which science is constantly approaching. Could God actually *do* anything in our world? This question is also addressed in this chapter, and my answer is used, directly or indirectly, in much of the rest of the book.

3. I will defer the discussion of a final question—for many persons the most difficult one—to the book's Appendix 2. That is the question of whether any God who existed at all could be both powerful and good, considering all the pain and evil in the world. Assertive answers to this question are called theodicies. I present some ideas that help me to wrestle with the question, but I do not propose a rigorous theodicy.

Religious Experience and Scientific Experience

I myself sometimes engage the thought that religion in general, and Christianity in particular, may be "all in our heads." One argument opposing that view does have a fairly objective base: a number of physical constants describing our universe have values, each of which lies in a very important range—a range in which it must fall in order for humans to exist. (For example, the percentage of the total energy that is released when hydrogen is fused into helium, allowing the sun to keep on shining, needs to be within a very small range of all possible values, or the world we know couldn't exist.) Why, we wonder, is that?

In his book, *Just Six Numbers: The Deep Forces That Shape the Universe*, Sir Martin Rees, British Astronomer Royal, describes two possible answers to that question, answers that attribute that fact to the outcome of the operation of pure chance and nothing more (Rees, 2000, pp. 166–171). First, it is possible that, as some have suggested, scientists will someday discover that a universe "fine-tuned" for sentient life in this way is the only kind of universe that could possibly exist. (I consider that unlikely, and if it should eventually turn out to be true, I would wonder how it could be true "just by accident.") Alternatively, it is possible that our universe is just one of a multitude of universes, the vast majority of which could not support life of any sort that is remotely similar to ours.

To me it seems much likelier that this universe is *the* universe, period, and that it was deliberately constructed in a way that would allow sentient life forms to arise. My support for this conclusion, which agrees with one form of the so-called "strong anthropic principle," is based on more than my belief in God. In evaluating contrasting explanations of phenomena, scientists generally tend to put some weight on "Occam's [or Ockham's] Razor." In the fourteenth century, William of Ockham put forth "the logical principle that the simplest possible explanation for a phenomenon should be adopted" (Wilcox, 1975, p. 258). It seems to me that that criterion would favor one intended universe over myriads of universes that somehow just happened. The fact that those six numbers to which Rees referred are all in just the right ranges for this kind of universe to be possible is in my view hard evidence—certainly not proof, but good, objective evidence—that this universe was willed to be the way it is. That is, the *likeliest* way, in my view, to understand why there is a planet in our universe on which humanity could develop is also the *simplest* way: namely to understand it as a universe in which sentient, living forms of some sort or sorts were intended to develop. (I will use the word *likeliest* many times in this book. Mathematicians can prove their main theorems, but scientists cannot in general prove their main conclusions; they must instead always seek the likeliest explanations for the data available at the moment. In dealing with the topics I will discuss, the latter course is necessary.)

More broadly, however, discussions usually contrast religious beliefs with scientific beliefs in regard to the subjective nature of the former as compared to the objective nature of the latter. The contrast stems from the need in religion to rely on personal experiences, whereas experiences in the "hard" sciences, such as reading a dial or measuring a distance, are believed to have no essential role in shaping what occurs. The experimental scientist is seen as primarily a recorder, and the theoretician develops ways to understand what the experimentalist records. Based in large part on that contrast, coupled with the manifold successes of scientific studies, many people regard scientific beliefs to be the only reliable way to truth about the nature of reality—the real world (or universe, really) that includes us but also everything else that is "really real."

I assert that although physics experiments and their analysis—that is, in the day-to-day experiences in the most fundamental science—are objective, they tell us much less about the physical world around us than it was thought they did in, say, 1900.

For centuries it was thought that physics provided us with increasingly better understanding of truths about the natural world itself, irrespective of the presence of humanity or any other kind of "observer." So great has been the progress of science that someone might suppose that physics, and its extensions into the other physical and biological sciences, would in fact ultimately bring us to an understanding of the full nature of reality—that there would be nothing left for religion to explain. Research done in recent decades, however, has shown that at the deepest level we have reached—the level of electrons, photons, and such entities—we are not learning about the natural world itself but rather about the ways in which humans can interact with that world. Truths about ultimate reality at the atomic and subatomic levels themselves, in other words, may well be largely beyond our reach.

Ideas of this sort have permeated the long-standing debates on what quantum mechanics, the field of physics that treats nature at those levels, really tells us.

In describing ideas that played a part in the so-called "Copenhagen interpretation of quantum mechanics," physicist Henry P. Stapp beautifully expressed the basic problem this way:

> [I]deas and external realities are presumably very different kinds of things. Our ideas are intimately associated with certain complex, macroscopic, biological entities—our brains—and the structural forms that can inhere in our ideas would naturally be expected to depend on the structural forms of our brains. External realities, on the other hand, could be structurally very different from human ideas. Hence there is no *a priori* reason to expect that relationships that constitute or characterize the essence of external reality can be mapped in any simple or direct fashion into the world of human ideas. Yet if no such mapping exists then the whole idea of "agreement" between ideas and external realities becomes obscure. (Stapp, 1972, p. 1104)

In recent decades, physics has continued to make enormous progress in finding ideas that provide consistent correlations among various atomic and subatomic phenomena. The concepts of quarks, gluons, and so on have been very successful ideas and certainly have something to do with external reality. This fact does not prove, however, that those ideas are "simple or direct" mappings of external realities. They may be less like objects than like the shadows of objects on complicated surfaces.

In a recent issue of *Physics Today*, the primary news magazine for physicists in the United States, David Mermin, retired Cornell University professor of physics, supported a key idea advanced by Niels Bohr, a leading twentieth-century quantum physicist and philosopher. Mermin commented,

> In my youth I had little sympathy for Niels Bohr's philosophical pronouncements. … [But] I've come to realize that buried in those ponderous documents are some real gems: "In our description of nature the purpose is not to disclose the real essence of the phenomena but only to track down, so far as it is possible, relations between the manifold aspects of our experience," and "Physics is to be regarded not so much as the study of something a priori given [that is, the physical world itself], but rather as the development of methods for

> ordering and surveying human experience." (Mermin, 2009, p. 9)

Here is an example that illustrates Bohr's point. You may have heard about "wave-particle duality," an atomic-level phenomenon in which particles of matter (such as electrons) and particles of light (photons) each display, in certain experimental arrangements, wavelike characteristics, as if they could pass through two different openings at once, as a wave easily does; *and yet* they each display particle-like characteristics in other experimental arrangements. Researchers working with photons have noted the possibility of what is called a "delayed choice" experiment, in which particle-like behavior (passing through only one slit) or wavelike behavior (passing simultaneously through two slits) is not determined until *after* a photon has already landed on a screen located beyond the slits.

The reason deals with the probabilistic nature of how we are able to describe photons: a photon's physical properties can be probabilistically "entangled" with those of a second photon. In a delayed choice experiment, after one photon marks a detection screen, a decision can be made as to what property of a second, entangled photon to measure. That decision determines whether the first one is part of an ensemble of other photons that shows particle-like behavior or part of an ensemble of still other photons that shows wavelike behavior. To quote a description of the proposed experiment appearing in the magazine *American Scientist*, "All [my measurements] told me was how to divide up [the] experimental results" in order to show either type of behavior (Walborn, S. P. et al, 2003, p. 343).

So, did the photon *really* go through just one slit, like a particle, or through both, like a wave? The question is apparently invalid. Our whole notion of the photon having either a sharply defined location or a widely defined location through a region in which it is not detected has failed to describe this situation. Photons are, in some sense, a real component of the physical world, but our concept of a trajectory—giving the location of an object (be it a wave or a particle) as a function of time—is not working in this situation.

This notion, that a physical concept as fundamental as location has limitations in its applicability to physical systems, brings to mind the other great twentieth-century innovation in physics: the introduction of relativity theory in two forms. Here is a comment by Albert Einstein, founder of both the special form and the general form: "After seven years of reflection in vain, the solution came to me suddenly with the thought that our concepts and laws of space and time can only claim validity insofar as they stand in a clear relation to our experiences; and that experience could very well lead to the alteration of these concepts and laws" (Einstein, as quoted by Rigden, 2005, p. 85).

Such was the case with his theories of relativity. His special theory, which came out in 1905, connects time and space in a more intricate way than was previously expected, and his general theory of 1915 reinterprets gravity in an entirely new way. Both theories have withstood all tests so far made of them.

What does all this have to do with scientific knowledge at its most fundamental level? It means that all we can do is, as Bohr put it, study "relations between the manifold aspects of our experience." We cannot get at the "real essence of the phenomena" (Mermin, 2009, p. 9). As Stapp suggested, we conceive of the world only in ways permitted by our collective brains. The limitation this imposes introduces a subjective aspect to the objective explanations provided by science.

Of course, religious experience in this world is ultimately limited in much the same way. In his book *Religion in an Age of Science*, physicist and theologian Ian Barbour wrote: "We can ask how God is related to us, but we can say little about the intrinsic nature of God"

(Barbour, 1990, pp. 121–122). Religious experience is thus, in this important aspect, not entirely different from scientific experience at the most basic level. Granted, religious experiences are far more subjective than the experiences gained from experiments in physics, but both religion and science are human attempts to better understand human experiences as they relate to probably unreachable realities.

Bohr himself was not religious in the conventional sense, except during a brief period in his teenage years, according to physicist Abraham Pais's biography (Pais, 1991, p. 134). However, Bohr's thinking on many issues was complex and deep. His colleague Werner Heisenberg once reported his own recollections of a 1927 conversation about science and religion in which Bohr participated. According to Heisenberg, Bohr said something like this:

> Hence we conclude that if religion does indeed deal with objective truths, it ought to adopt the same criteria of truth as science. But I myself find the division of the world into an objective and a subjective side much too arbitrary. The fact that religions through the ages have spoken in images, parables, and

> paradoxes means simply that there are no other ways of grasping the reality to which they refer. But that does not mean that it is not a genuine reality. And splitting this reality into an objective and a subjective side won't get us very far. (Heisenberg, 1962, p. 18)

Heisenberg recalled that Bohr illustrated this point by the example of a divine intervention, saying something like this: "When we speak of divine intervention, we quite obviously do not refer to the scientific determination of an event, but to the meaningful connection between this event and others or human thought. Now this intellectual connection is as much a part of reality as scientific causality; it would be much too crude a simplification if we ascribed it [the intellectual connection to such an event] exclusively to the subjective side of reality" (Heisenberg, 1962, p. 23).

The Nature of the Laws of Nature

As suggested in the preface, I will argue later that in providing the appearances of Jesus, God affected the world as we know it in direct ways—by "divine intervention." In this section, I will argue that the laws of nature themselves permit that possibility.

First I need to clarify that what I mean by "divine intervention" goes beyond simply influencing the course of events. I am a strong believer in human free will, meaning that, in my opinion, our decisions are ultimately not determinable by science, nor are they determined by God. They are truly free choices that we make from among the possible options available to us. I believe that, all the time and among all of humanity, God hopes to shape the course of events by influencing—but not determining—which options we choose. This belief in the openness of the future underlies my approach to the religious and theological issues I address in the later parts of this book. My serious consideration of this line of thinking may have begun with readings in *God and the World* by process theologian John B. Cobb Jr. In that book, Cobb, following Alfred North Whitehead, wrote of God as *One Who Calls* us "so to actualize ourselves in [each] moment as to embody some ideal maximum of experience ..." (Cobb, 1969, p. 54). This call seeks to *persuade* us to choose paths leading toward ideal behavior; it is not coercive.

But can God actually make things happen—things that otherwise would definitely not have happened? This question goes beyond affecting the course of events by seeking to influence our actions. It asks whether God can also *change* the course of events directly, regardless of the true laws of nature.

Two issues need to be addressed in terms of the possibility of God taking direct action to shape the course of specific events in this universe (world). For clarity's sake, I will therefore divide the question into two parts, one dealing with law-*abiding*, direct action, and the other with law-*suspending* direct action.

1. Can God intervene without breaking the true laws of nature (those laws toward which science strives)?

A possible way to respond positively to this question is in terms of what has been termed a "God of the gaps" concept of God. An outcome that one would expect to be covered by the true laws of nature might not be so covered, thus indicating a gap in the laws' realm of applicability. The idea is, then, that God's ongoing, omnipresent action must be the explanation of that outcome and thus could be a way in which God has an active role in human experience. An early example of an attempt to use God to fill a gap left by science is Isaac Newton's belief that God needed to make occasional adjustments in the orbital motions of the planets in order to account for the solar system's stability. That is, Newton believed that the observed stability of the solar system was not covered by the laws of mechanics and the law of universal gravitation—although one would hope that it would be covered—and therefore that divine intervention was occasionally needed to keep the system stable.

However, Pierre-Simon Laplace showed that stability over long periods of time was, instead, guaranteed by those same laws, thus weakening the case for God as gap-filler. Incidentally, Laplace is famous for his response to Napoleon's question regarding how God was involved in the way the solar system operates. "I have no need of that hypothesis," Laplace answered. Less well-known is that at some time he expressed the following reflection: "But may not this disposition of the planets be itself an effect of the laws of motion: and may not the Supreme Intelligence, to whose intervention Newton had recourse, have made this orderly disposition dependent on a phenomenon of a more general character?" (Laplace, as cited in Jaki, 1966, p. 433). It would appear that Laplace was no atheist.

Some scientists tend to see the use of "God of the gaps" reasoning as the main reason for belief in God. Therefore, they doubt God's reality, since the alleged gaps keep being filled by science alone. However, this type of reasoning has, by and large, been discredited for decades by many theologians. The text of a book by Barbour, entitled *Issues in Science and Religion* and published in 1966, states on the very first page that "[t]he 'God of the gaps,' invoked [in recent centuries] as a hypothesis to account for scientifically unexplained facts, or introduced as a cause producing effects on the same level as natural causes, retreated further as each of the gaps in human knowledge was closed. But in addition such a picture of God had little relevance to the religious life [and so] was as dubious from the standpoint of religion as from that of science" (Barbour, 1966, p. 1).

Recent positive answers to the question of whether God could act directly in our times without breaking a true law of nature avoid the God-of-the-gaps categorization. These answers arise from metaphysical approaches in which God takes advantage of the probabilistic nature of quantum physics. A little more background is needed to understand this feature.

Physicists understand how the dot made by an electron impacting a detection screen *can have* occurred—the probability of its landing in that region of the screen was not zero—but most of them would disagree that the electron *had* to land in that region. Thus there seems to be a lack of "determinacy" at the most fundamental levels of the physical universe that we have reached experimentally. Many physicists consider the successes of the probabilistic laws of quantum mechanics to show that at the atomic level and below, nature itself is *inherently, fundamentally* probabilistic. Only the pattern made by thousands of such dots necessarily has to have a certain appearance according to the laws of quantum mechanics, most physicists would say. (The way this idea is applied to an individual electron is to assume that it is fundamentally described by a "wave function" that, in accordance with a certain law, allows one to calculate the *relative probability* that the electron can be detected in a given region of space at a given time.)

William Pollard, a highly respected physicist and an Episcopal priest, wrote numerous books on the relationships between science and religion. As noted by Barbour, Pollard discussed the randomness of physical processes at the atomic level "as a possible sphere" for the activity of God: the outcome of some particular atomic-level event that is seen by the scientific world as due to chance, "the Christian can look on … as a place where God's *providential control* is exercised. … [In so doing,] God determines only which actual value among the naturally determined probabilities is to occur" (Barbour, 1966, p. 428).

Pollard's approach does not use a God-of-the-gaps methodology, as long as the probabilistic nature of quantum mechanics is taken to be a fundamental feature of nature. Barbour explains this reasoning more explicitly: God is not envisioned as having to apply some force similar to that of an electric field; nor does God have to "intervene to manipulate 'natural' probability patterns" (Barbour, 1966, p. 429). That is, the proposed activity of God does not fill a gap at the same level as, or within the scope of, natural law; it lies beyond that scope. It does not add to our scientific account of the universe but is instead a faith-based conjecture about activity beyond that with which science deals. It is theology, not science.

Pollard used this approach to argue for divine sovereignty as "total control over the world" (Barbour, 1966, p. 429). Barbour opposed this idea, writing that it "seems … incompatible with human freedom and the reality of evil" (Barbour, 1990, p. 117). Recent scholars—including Robert Russell, professor of theology and science in residence at the Graduate Theological Union—have advocated a view in which God "influences *only certain quantum events* and also acts at higher levels as a top-down cause on events at lower levels" (Barbour, 2000, p. 87).

In this quote, the verb "influences" is a little weak in regard to Russell's more recently published *Cosmology: From Alpha to Omega*. There, Russell puts his point this way: "I am claiming theologically that God acts together with nature to determine which quantum outcome becomes actual by providing what nature lacks as an efficient cause and that God does so without being a natural cause, efficient or otherwise. In essence, God can know which potential state will become actual since *God causes it to become actual!*" (Russell, 2008, p. 171).

Russell's metaphysics is thus in this respect a gentler version of Pollard's. Pollard had God determining all events, and Russell has God determining only certain events.

Some very accomplished physicists, following Einstein's lead, feel that someday a theory more fundamental than quantum mechanics will be found, one that will ground the probabilistic successes of quantum mechanics in a deeper, deterministic base. In that case, the idea of direct divine intervention will lose the defense that basic laws determine only probabilities of outcomes. Unless and until that happens, Russell and Pollard must be considered possibly correct in answering the question, "Can God intervene without breaking the 'true' laws of nature (those laws toward which science strives)?," with the response, "Yes, because God can determine outcomes different from those that otherwise would be determined purely by the laws of probability."

2. Can God intervene by suspending, at will, the operation of the true laws of nature, whatever they are?

I believe there is a God who is directly or indirectly responsible for the operation of this universe, including the phenomena that *normally* follow true laws of nature, but that this God is not limited by those laws—that the God responsible for their creation could suspend their application at will. In the nineteenth century Sir George Stokes—the discoverer of the law of fluid resistance that bears his name—put it this way: "Admit the existence of God, of a personal God, and the possibility of miracles follows at once; if the laws of nature are carried on in accordance with His will, He Who willed them may will their suspension." (as cited in Jaki, 1966, p. 453)

Stokes then added the following sentence. "And if any difficulty should be felt as to their suspension, we are not even obliged to suppose that they have been suspended." I presume that he meant this sentence to refer to the fact that what we currently know about the laws of nature may be a very long way from the true laws.

And it is true that the true laws of nature *could* allow results that affect the world here and now in ways that people could directly experience and yet could never explain by humanly devised laws of nature. In the next subsection, I will present my view that that option is not, in my view, the likeliest way to explain the alleged appearances of Jesus, if they did in fact occur.

I endorse the *first* sentence quoted from Stokes as the best way to understand those alleged appearances.

Support for this conclusion is provided by a close look at the nature of the laws of nature, as best we can understand them. As suggested in the first part of this chapter, what physics—the foundational science—helps us to realize is that *the most our science can describe is how, in humanly designed investigations using humanly developed concepts, the things of nature normally behave.* Science combines logical thinking with experimentation to decide among various possible ways of explaining observed patterns of phenomena, but there is no way to argue, within science itself, that all phenomena must fit those patterns. And even if they did, there is no way to argue, within science itself, that they *must* be explained in those ways. As historian Will Durant has described, the eighteenth century philosopher David Hume pointed out that "we never perceive causes, or laws; we perceive events and sequences, and *infer* causation and necessity; a law is not an eternal and necessary decree to which events are subjected, but merely a mental summary and shorthand of our kaleidoscopic experience …" (Durant, 1953, p. 258).

There is a common tendency to assume that, since our best approximations to the true laws of nature describe so well what happens, the true laws of nature describe what must happen. Why does a pen fall when you release it? Because, we tend to say, it *must* fall. The combination of Newton's law of gravity and his laws of motion imply—in agreement with Einstein's more widely applicable general theory of relativity—that the pen must now accelerate downward. This is faulty logic, because it misrepresents what humanly devised laws of nature tell us. Years ago, in a letter to the editor of *Science News*—a letter not dealing with religious matters—P. M. deLaubenfels described the role of nature's laws as follows: "The laws of physics are descriptive, not prescriptive. They do not 'allow' anything [nor, I would add, do they "prohibit" anything] … We sometimes tend to forget this fact about 'laws' of nature" (deLaubenfels,1992, p. 411). The fact that, eighteen years later, this author felt the need to remind us *again* that "the laws [of physics] only describe nature" (deLaubenfels, 2010, p. 34) illustrates the pervasiveness of our tendency to think otherwise.

Specific Considerations

My main interest here in Part 1 of this book is the question of whether divine intervention is the likeliest explanation of certain post-crucifixion appearances of Jesus, assuming for the present that they did in fact occur. We do not know the precise nature of the appearances, but at the minimum they each involved a vision carrying a message, a revelation. My purpose in this subsection is to explain my belief that such an event could not have happened purely by chance, that it must have been intended. In a later chapter, I will present my case that some appearances were not likely to have been self-produced by the persons who reported them, either.

I will make the claim here that, in this specific case, it does not matter whether nature is fundamentally probabilistic or not. If it is, then the true laws of probability, whatever they are, would ascribe a probability of virtually zero for those events to have occurred. That is to say: if they occurred, it is virtually impossible to believe that they occurred by pure chance. And on the other hand, if nature at its core is deterministic, I will argue that it would still be virtually impossible to believe that those events could occur without having been intended. Almost anything, of course, is possible, but I think that the likeliest explanation of the post-crucifixion appearances of Jesus, if in fact they occurred, is that God deliberately suspended the normal operation of the relevant laws. My basis for that belief, in spite of my having no knowledge about the true laws of nature, is the way in which science in general and physics in particular develop. Here's my argument.

From a scientific point of view, regardless of whether the true laws of nature are probabilistic, *we should expect the currently known laws—imperfect as they are—to give correct descriptions at the everyday level at which our lives are lived.* The relationship between Einstein's general relativity theory and Newton's theory of universal gravitation can serve to illustrate this fact.

Einstein's theory is both a broader and deeper theory than Newton's. In addition to explaining things that lie outside the realm of Newton's theory—such as the fact that a clock runs slower when placed in a stronger gravitational field—Einstein's theory gives us a deeper way to understand things like the orbits of planets around the sun. But Einstein's achievements do not change the fact that planets follow the orbits they do—orbits that, by and large, Newton's laws explain with high, although not perfect, precision. No relativity theory is needed in the prediction of the particular minute when, on some particular day, the planet Jupiter will rise at some specific location. And no new theory will predict a different minute for its rising.

In the same way, successors to quantum mechanics may give us a deeper understanding (maybe still probabilistic, maybe not) of why the probabilities of atomic-level events are what they are, but the probability of some chosen electron striking a detecting screen in some specified region will still be almost exactly what it is calculated to be by quantum mechanics … even if it is guided there by some deterministic (but natural) influence. The pattern on the screen that emerges after thousands of electrons have been detected will still be what it is; no improvement or replacement of quantum mechanics is going to predict a noticeably different pattern on the screen. For practical human purposes, that fact boils down to the same probability, as can be predicted now, for any given electron to land in any specified region of the screen.

And here's the point: from a purely scientific perspective, Jesus' crucifixion was a not-uncommon biophysical and biochemical series of events, and such series are not normally followed by post-execution appearances. Just as the probability of Jupiter rising, under normal circumstances, an hour later than our astronomical laws predict is virtually zero, the probability that, *without the action of either human or divine will*, the biological features of a human brain could produce the alleged post-crucifixion appearances of Jesus is virtually zero—regardless of whether the true laws of nature are fundamentally probabilistic.

Conclusions

Regardless of the precise nature of the true laws of nature, I am convinced that (a) God can intervene in the natural course of events, and (b) the natural course of events did not lead to the post-crucifixion appearances of Jesus, if they did in fact occur. These conclusions play key roles in Chapters 4, 5, and 7. In Chapter 4, I will use them to argue that the likeliest explanation of the alleged post-crucifixion appearances of Jesus is that God did so intervene, interrupting the normal operation of those laws. That explanation of the appearances is the context in which Chapter 5 is developed, and I will use that conclusion again in Chapter 7 in discussing some alleged acts of Jesus and the early Christians.

2

About the Focus of Jesus' Teaching

Narrowing the Big Picture

For many Christians, the big picture of Christianity is this: while the teachings of Jesus as presented in the Synoptic Gospels—those attributed to Matthew, Mark, and Luke—are important, they are not central to the gospel, the "good news" that lies at the core of the faith. That gospel—revealed after Jesus' resurrection to Paul and elaborated primarily in his letters and in John's gospel—says that through Jesus' death and resurrection we can be reconciled to God, leading to abundant life on this side of the grave and eternal life on the other side. While I agree with that gospel—I will refer to it as "Paul's gospel" later—I believe that what it covers is just the tip of the iceberg. To me, the rest of the iceberg is the message Jesus provided, through word and deed, before his death: Jesus' own good news. In my opinion, his gospel provides a way to be reconciled with God that is itself inherent to the abundant life in the here-and-now.

Thus I must make a major assumption at the outset in dealing with the belief that, by producing the post-resurrection appearances, God validated the most relevant part of "Jesus' own gospel." By that phrase, I mean his message as portrayed in those Synoptic Gospels—I will call them by the names traditionally associated with them—in which he focuses mostly on the "kingdom of God," not his message as portrayed in the gospel of John, in which the primary emphases do not include God's kingdom. This choice agrees with that of many modern scholars, but it is a choice. And making that choice means that I will not be discussing, in any detail, much of what many Christians consider to be the crux of the Christian faith: namely, what to believe about the nature and the role of Jesus the Christ beyond his presence as a teacher and healer in the world of the first century CE. Nor will I have much to say, except in an appendix, about conceptions of life beyond death, which to some are key features of the faith. I will discuss what Jesus seems to me to have taught about the nature of God as God relates to *this* world, and in particular about the "kingdom" that Jesus said was beginning to be established in this world. First, however, I will use evidence that is generally accepted as factual as the basis of my conclusion that God intended the teachings of Jesus to be a central focus of Christianity.

Some fairly recent books have considered this idea already. For example, in *The Scandalous Gospel of Jesus*, Peter Gomes, the late Pusey Minister of the Memorial Church at Harvard University, wrote that "[i]n our zeal to crown [Jesus] as the content of our preaching, most of us have failed to give due deference to the content of his preaching" (Gomes, 2007, p.17). In this book, I hope to be faithful to what—as best we can reconstruct it—Jesus taught about the kingdom of God on earth.

There also, however, I must deal with some degree of uncertainty. Although many scholars agree that the kingdom of God was Jesus' primary concern, they are to some considerable extent divided on how heavily Jesus emphasized the nature of the "in-breaking" of God's kingdom into the world as we know it, as opposed to the nature of an apocalyptic, end-of-the-world-as-we-know-it, full-scale arrival of the kingdom. Norman Perrin, a leading New Testament scholar of the twentieth century, expressed the difference in these approaches in terms of whether Jesus focused on the end of the world as a gradual approach to the kind of world God works to achieve or as a physical event happening worldwide at a particular time. He characterized "apocalyptic" writing as that which claims "that God had revealed to the writer the secrets of the imminent end of the world and so had given him a message for his people" (Perrin, 1974, p.65).

In the next part of this chapter, I discuss the importance of deciding to focus either on the apocalyptic or on the non-apocalyptic Scriptures attributed to Jesus, and I will explain my preference for focusing on the non-apocalyptic Scriptures. Then in the third part of the chapter, I will discuss a way in which both types of Scripture can possibly be ascribed to Jesus as major emphases.

In closing this section, I should make a few comments about the gospel of John, since it is so important a source for Christian theology. I see it much as does Stephen L. Harris of the California State University at Sacramento, who wrote in his textbook, *Understanding the Bible*: "The Gospel of John is so different from the Synoptics that most scholars conclude that it is fundamentally not a portrait of the historical Jesus, but a profound meditation on his theological significance" (Harris, 2000, p. 413).

Citing John 20:31, Harris notes, "The author clearly states his purpose: to inspire faith in Jesus' divinity" (Harris, 2000, p. 414). As suggested above, my book focuses on what the man Jesus said and did in the first century, as best we can surmise.

Apocalyptic or Not Apocalyptic?

The Synoptic Gospels include numerous apocalyptic passages and numerous non-apocalyptic passages; and the two types are quite different in tone and emphasis. Understandably, many biblical scholars believe that, for the most part if not entirely, Jesus taught one type or the other, not both. A complicating factor is that there is good evidence that, from the outset, what was spoken or written in later decades about what Jesus taught was often influenced by persons who were more intent on advancing the Christian faith as they saw it than on preserving historical accuracy.

Bart Ehrman, a biblical scholar at the University of North Carolina at Chapel Hill, has written extensively on that evidence. It is probable, as Ehrman has claimed, that "before anyone bothered to *write* stories about Jesus, they had circulated by word of mouth for years and years" and "[a]s the stories circulated orally, they were changed to suit the purposes at hand. And they were modified yet further when they were written down in such lost documents as Q and further still when rewritten by the authors of our gospels" (Ehrman, 1999, p. 87).

What were those "purposes at hand"? Scholars tend to agree that the views of the Christian church in its earliest days were strongly apocalyptic. The Jewish people at the time of Jesus' crucifixion had been suffering under Roman domination for some time, and so were looking to God for release from that oppression. It is likely, then, that the Jews who at the outset formed the Christian movement's base were at least somewhat familiar with scriptural prophecies of an eternal kingdom established when God gives "everlasting dominion" to "one like a son of man" (Daniel 7:13–14). Moreover, in Daniel 12:2, a general resurrection of the dead was also predicted; and before the gospels were written, Paul had affirmed Jesus as "firstfruits" of that general resurrection that was to occur at the close of the age (1 Corinthians 15:20), which Paul thought was about to happen. These ideas fit well with the belief that a second coming of Jesus was imminent.

Thus it could be expected that bearers of oral traditions in the first decades of the Christian Era would tend to place accounts of Jesus' own sayings in apocalyptic settings, especially if, as may often have happened, the original contexts of the sayings of Jesus had been lost. Robert Funk and Roy Hoover, writing for the Jesus Seminar, have emphasized that this solution to forgotten contexts continued to the gospel writers themselves, in the time period of approximately 70 to 100 CE (Funk et al., 1997, p. 21). The majority of scholars in the Jesus Seminar thus considered the apocalyptic portions of the gospels as products of the early Christian movement.

Ehrman, on the other hand, considers the apocalyptic material in the gospels to give the most reliable picture of what Jesus taught. He points out that our earliest written sources of information, namely the gospel of Mark and the document called "Q," which although lost is widely believed to have provided much material to the Synoptic Gospels, are both heavily apocalyptic. Moreover, Ehrman claims that the later gospels (especially John and the recently discovered gospel of Thomas) were influenced by a turning away from the apocalyptic: "some of the most clearly apocalyptic traditions come to be 'toned down' as we move further away from Jesus' life in the 20s to Gospel materials produced near the end of the first century" (Ehrman, 1999, p. 130).

Therefore a basic question arises: To what extent does the apocalyptic material ascribed to Jesus in the Synoptic Gospels reflect his words, and to what extent does it reflect the desire of the gospel writers or their predecessors or successors to convert others to a Christianity focused on the second coming? How we answer that general question greatly affects our understanding of biblical material, as can be shown by the following two examples.

1. Chapter 13 of the gospel of Mark is highly apocalyptic. In verse 4, the writer had followers asking Jesus what signs would indicate the coming of the events that end the age. Jesus provided a lengthy response, including the signs that the sun and moon would become dark and stars would fall from heaven (vv. 24–25). Afterward, the Son of Man would come in the clouds to gather the righteous (vv. 26–27), and Jesus stated that "this generation will not pass away before all these things have taken place" (v. 30).

Ehrman considers these verses as probably originating, not in the bearers of oral traditions or by the writers of Mark and Q, but in Jesus' own teaching. He asserts that Mark 13 provides Jesus' "most explicitly apocalyptic message," which was delivered in the temple in Jerusalem "according to all three of the Synoptic Gospels …" (Ehrman, 1999, p. 214). However, the consensus of the scholars in the Jesus Seminar felt that Mark 13 came from the early Christian church, one source being the gospel's writer himself (Funk et al., 1997, pp. 107–108).

2. Luke 17:20–21 has Jesus proclaiming that the kingdom is not coming with visible signs. Once Jesus was asked by the Pharisees when the kingdom of God was coming, and he answered, "The kingdom of God is not coming with things that can be observed; nor will they say, "Look, here it is!' or 'There it is!' For, in fact, the kingdom of God is among [or within] you."

Perrin cited the words attributed to Jesus in these verses as one of the sayings that are almost certain to be authentic (Perrin, 1974, p. 289), and the Jesus Seminar scholars felt that this saying is "a key in identifying Jesus' temporal views" (Funk et al., 1997, p. 364). Ehrman, however, uses the saying as an example of a toning-down of some apocalyptic traditions by later gospel writers, noting that the verse appears only in the gospel of Luke, "a gospel … that went some way to tone down the apocalyptic dimensions of our earlier sources" (Ehrman, 1999, p. 177).

In defense of Luke 17:20–21, it is by no means clear that attributions to Jesus' teaching that are found *only* in Matthew or *only* in Luke were essentially created by those authors. In fact, the Jesus Seminar decided that this passage most likely came from "Q," which, along with Mark's gospel, is considered to be as early as any available to us. (If it was in Q, presumably Matthew considered it as too much in contradiction to the apocalyptic passages he was including in his gospel to include it as well.) Moreover the scholars in the Jesus Seminar consider a passage in the recently discovered gospel of Thomas—passage 113—to be close enough to Luke 17:20–21 to be considered an independent attribution. It is also possible that Luke's source for the passage was a source called "L," of material found only in Luke's gospel. Funk and Hoover note that the material contained in "L" and in "M" (defined as a source of material found only in Matthew's gospel) "probably comes from oral tradition" (Funk et al., 1997, p. 15).

Ehrman himself discusses how little we know about L and M: "It is generally assumed that the gospel writers didn't make up these stories [categorized as L or M] whole-cloth (they certainly *may* have; but given their use of other sources for their accounts, it seems somewhat unlikely). If not, then they must have gotten them from someplace—either written documents that no longer survive or oral traditions that they had heard ... Since these sources also predated the gospels into which they were incorporated, they, too, could provide early access to the sayings and deeds of Jesus" (Ehrman, 1999, pp. 82–83). Thus the verses in Luke 17:20–21 could well represent something Jesus said.

Luke—and Matthew—clearly did "de-apocalypticize" some of the apocalyptic material in Mark. For example, as Ehrman points out, references to Christ's second coming attributed to Jesus were made less specific (Ehrman, 1999, pp. 130, 131). The Jesus Seminar scholars also note signs of this revising (Funk et al., 1997, p. 209). An obvious explanation for such revisions is that the gospels of Matthew and Luke were written a considerable time after that of Mark—perhaps fifteen to twenty years later—and a second coming had still not happened. However, those considerations do not necessarily take us farther away from things that Jesus actually said in every instance. Mark and the author of Q, writing some decades into the development of the Christian movement, may have added apocalyptic frameworks or in other ways "apocalypticized" some of the earliest recollections of Jesus' teachings in order to reinforce their theme. Ehrman implies that this is a possibility in the book *Forged: Writing in the Name of God: Why the Bible's Authors Are Not Who We Think They Are.* He writes,

> Many Jews expected that in the future God would fulfill his promise to David and bring a new anointed one, a new "messiah" to rule his people Israel. The gospels are written to show that in fact this new messiah is none other than Jesus … To be sure, Jesus was different from the kind of messiah that other Jews were expecting. Rather than coming as a great king, like David, he came as a prophet speaking of the *future* kingdom of God. He himself would bring this kingdom not by being installed as king in Jerusalem, but by dying on the cross to bring salvation. This was a salvation not from … the Romans, but from the ultimate enemies of God, the powers of sin and death. Jesus conquered these alien powers at his death and resurrection, and he is returning soon as king of the earth.

> This is the message of the gospels, and it is portrayed in these books as continuous with the anonymously written history of Israel as laid out in the Old Testament Scriptures. (Ehrman, 2011, p. 224)

Thus, both toning-down ("de-apocalypticizing") *and* "apocalypticizing" can be inferred as possibilities. A good overview is provided in Ehrman's *From Jesus to Constantine: A History of Early Christianity, Part I.* "To sum it up, the religion of Jesus became the religion about Jesus as soon as his followers came to believe that Jesus had been raised from the dead. Then, they began to call him the Son of Man, the Son of God, the Messiah, the Lord, and they told stories about him, stories that changed in the process of transmission, and were eventually written down by different people at different times who had different perspectives" (Ehrman, 2004, p. 70).

It is interesting that a particular simile is considered by Ehrman to be an example of Jesus' apocalyptic teachings, while it is considered by the Jesus Seminar to reflect authentically what Jesus probably said. Ehrman interprets the parable of the mustard seed (Mark 4:30–32) as Jesus' way of emphasizing what an enormous change will be experienced at the coming day of judgment (Ehrman, 1999, p. 179). The Jesus Seminar, on the other hand, interprets the passage in its original form as Jesus using a garden herb to poke fun at grandiose images such as "the apocalyptic tree of Daniel" (Funk et al., 1997, pp. 194–95). How did *Jesus* mean for this simile to be interpreted? Nobody knows!

The debate over the authenticity of apocalyptic attributions to Jesus has a long history. Decades ago, in the textbook for my college course in the New Testament, D. W. Beck of Syracuse University contrasted the views of Albert Schweitzer and C. H. Dodd. To Schweitzer, Jesus was an apocalyptic prophet, whereas Dodd stressed "the present aspects of God's purposes in the field of human affairs" (D. W. Beck, 1954, p. 289). Beck himself advocated a middle-of-the-road answer.

> Jesus had definite ideas about the future for himself, his disciples, the temple [the destruction of which he predicted], his nation, the end of the age, and the part God would take in everything. He accepted some of the apocalyptic figures of speech, but he was not bewitched by them. He did not proclaim his teachings by visions. He was a prophet, not an apocalyptist. He believed that there were both present and future aspects to God's activity …

> He had the practical purpose to prepare his disciples for the future and to equip them with an attitude of watchfulness and faith and readiness for the future. (Beck, 1954, p. 289)

In *The Secret Message of Jesus,* Brian McLaren, a current leader in the "emerging church" movement, takes a position similar to Beck's, writing that phrases describing the moon turning to blood and stars falling from the sky are "rather typical stock phrases in Jewish apocalyptic" language, which would not have been taken any more seriously than would be comments in our day about "earth-shattering" election results (McLaren, 2006, p. 178).

Regarding an apocalyptic emphasis or a non-apocalyptic one: does it really make any significant difference? It does, because it determines whether we should believe that, at the time he gave his life, Jesus wanted his followers to give away everything and watch and wait for the cataclysmic events of the end of the age, as many of his later followers through the centuries have done. This is Ehrman's response, written near the end of *Jesus: Apocalyptic Prophet of the New Millennium.* He indicates that Jesus believed that "[t]he end of the world as we know it was already at hand. The Son of Man would soon arrive, bringing condemnation and judgment against those who prospered in this age, but salvation and justice to the poor, downtrodden, and oppressed. People should sacrifice everything for his coming, lest they be caught unawares and cast out of the kingdom that was soon to arrive" (Ehrman, 1999, p. 244).

Such an approach calls for followers to take drastic action, driven by fear, not by love, and it promotes a complete disregard for the state of affairs of planet Earth, for life as we know it is considered to be virtually over … for everybody. There is also a downside to the message that we are to deliberately become poor in the effort to please God. If life as we know it is about to end, then impoverishing ourselves by giving all we have to others provides no lasting benefits to those in need; and since it is intended to improve our chances to make it into heaven, such an action is therefore primarily self-serving.

Ehrman asserted that for Jesus righteous living in this world does in itself give a *foretaste* of "the coming kingdom, which would be brought in by a final judgment through the imminent appearance of the Son of Man" (Ehrman, 1999, pp. 176–77), but in his opinion, Jesus' message was not focused on life in this world, a world

Jesus thought was about to undergo a cataclysmic transformation.

I am certainly not a New Testament scholar, but if it is necessary to choose one type of message or another, it seems to me that Perrin and the Jesus Seminar had it right. One reason that I have not yet mentioned is that in *Parable and Gospel*, a posthumous collection of Perrin's works, Perrin had written that Richard A. Edwards, a student of his, had provided a strong case for the authenticity of a short passage in Mark (Perrin, 2003, p. 32). The passage reads: "The Pharisees came and began to argue with [Jesus], asking him for a sign from heaven, to test him. And he sighed deeply in his spirit and said, 'Why does this generation ask for a sign? Truly I tell you, no sign will be given to this generation.' And he left them, and getting into the boat again, he went across to the other side" (Mark 8:11–13). This directly contradicts those portions of Matthew 24, Mark 13, and Luke 21 that have Jesus predicting signs from heaven preceding the apocalypse.

Next, it is appropriate to examine the implications of the possibility that Jesus taught both apocalyptically and non-apocalyptically.

The Likelier Scenario, in My View, If the Teachings of Jesus Changed

Perrin wrote that in his view "all apocalyptic Son of Man sayings fail the test of the criteria for authenticity of sayings of Jesus ..., while at the same time exhibiting typical characteristics of early Christian prophecy" (Perrin, 1974, p. 77). About twenty years later, the Jesus Seminar scholars agreed: "John the Baptist, not Jesus, was the chief advocate of an impending cataclysm, a view that Jesus' first disciples had acquired from the Baptist movement. Jesus himself rejected that mentality in its crass form, quit the ascetic desert, and returned to urban Galilee" (Funk et al., 1997, p. 4).

And yet Ehrman states that in his opinion "the members of the Jesus Seminar typically got precisely wrong what Jesus actually said" (Ehrman, 2011, p. 246). In *Jesus: Apocalyptic Prophet of the New Millennium,* Ehrman makes a strong case in support of the hypothesis that Jesus thought and spoke of an apocalyptic end of this world as imminent, whereas a number of scholars, including Perrin and the members of the Jesus Seminar, have good reasons to support the alternative. Since there are good arguments on both sides of the debate, I wonder whether both sides may be right in some way.

The alternative to that hypothesis is difficult for me to accept. It is hard for me, on one hand, to believe that Mark or some earlier Christian decided to *create* the apocalyptic thirteenth chapter of that book and attribute it to Jesus. And on the other hand, although I agree that Luke often toned down the apocalyptic words attributed to Jesus in Mark, it is hard for me to believe that Luke or some predecessor decided to *create* the parables of the good Samaritan and the prodigal son and to indicate that Jesus had told them. Ehrman, in fact, feels somewhat likewise in regard to those parables (Ehrman, 1999, pp. 82–83). Might there be other options?

One alternative, mentioned by Ehrman, is that the apocalyptic language attributed to Jesus was "completely metaphorical" (Ehrman, 1999, p. 177). Ehrman naturally disagrees with the idea that Jesus used apocalyptic imagery metaphorically, whereas for the most part, the Jesus Seminar scholars disagree that Jesus used such language much at all. As mentioned early on, I tend to support Beck's view that Jesus used "some of the apocalyptic figures of speech, but he was not bewitched by them. He did not proclaim his teachings by visions" (Beck, 1954, p. 289).

On the other hand, the apocalyptic discourse in Mark 13, for example, seems quite visionary. If it is not purely a construction originating in the early Christian movement, is there some authentic kernel traceable back to things Jesus might have said? Noting that Mark 13 "has much more apocalyptic imagery than is usual in the teachings of Jesus," Beck added that some scholars have proposed that this discourse, as we have it, developed over time from a misinterpretation, namely that by "these things" Jesus meant "the end of Jerusalem," not that of the world (Beck, 1954, p. 293).

Along that line of thought, McLaren discusses the possibility that the apocalyptic material attributed to Jesus is, quite generally, not about the end of the world but is a metaphorical prediction along the lines of: "The temple will be destroyed. Jerusalem will fall. *Jewish* life as we know it will end" (McLaren, 2006, p. 179, emphasis added). Nevertheless, as Ehrman states, "[T]he fact is that there are apocalyptic pronouncements throughout all of our earliest accounts of Jesus' teachings" (Ehrman, 1999, p. 177), and to consider them *all* as metaphorical is a tall order.

Maybe Jesus was either schizophrenic or just could not decide what to emphasize about the coming of God's kingdom, and so he constantly alternated between emphasizing one approach and emphasizing the other. Neither of those options sounds right to me.

Another possible reason for the mixture of messages is that, during the course of his ministry, Jesus shifted his emphasis from one to the other, and while the different types of proclamations were both preserved, the order of examples of each type got jumbled in the process of transmission. This possibility would require that Jesus' understanding of God's will changed, irrespective of whether God's will itself changed or not. Regardless of the cause, Jesus would have shifted the emphasis of his message either toward a wrathful God about to condemn all sinners or toward a loving God having compassion even for sinners.

In one such scenario, Jesus would have decided at the outset of his ministry to distinguish his message from the apocalyptic message of John the Baptist, who by all accounts had baptized Jesus prior to the start of Jesus' own ministry. Later, under further reflection and guidance by God's Spirit, he would in this scenario have "come back to his roots," theologically speaking, and become an apocalyptic prophet like John before him.

In the opposite scenario, Jesus began his ministry under the tutelage of John the Baptist and preached apocalyptically in the early phase. Later, under further reflection and guidance by God's Spirit, he would have decided to emphasize the current in-breaking of God's kingdom.

Ehrman has considered the possibility that Jesus changed the emphasis of his message. He writes,

> There can be little doubt that Jesus went out into the wilderness to be baptized by [John the Baptist]. But why would he go? Since nobody compelled him, he must have gone to John, instead of to someone else, because he agreed with John's message. … That was how Jesus began. Is it possible, though, that he changed his views during the course of his ministry and began focusing on something other than what John preached? This is certainly possible, of course, but it would not explain why so many apocalyptic sayings are found on Jesus' own lips in the earliest sources for his life … Even more seriously, it would not explain what clearly emerged in the aftermath of his ministry. (Ehrman, 1999, pp. 138–9)

The last sentence quoted refers to the certainty that the early Christian movement was apocalyptic.

Early on, this quotation tends to support a switch from apocalyptic to non-apocalyptic—the scenario that seems more reasonable to me—but then it raises reasonable objections to it. In response to those objections, I would note the difficulty in explaining many of the parables and other non-apocalyptic sayings attributed to Jesus if he consistently preached apocalyptically.

Regarding his second objection, Ehrman goes on to say that "[t]he only connection between the apocalyptic John and the apocalyptic Christian church was Jesus himself" (Ehrman, 1999, p. 139). In response, I would note that the followers' belief in Jesus' *resurrection* (as opposed to his prior *teaching*) would seem to be more than sufficient motivation for the early church to adopt an apocalyptic message, when coupled with knowledge of apocalyptic passages in Daniel and/or recollections of what John the Baptist had preached. Jesus need not have been preaching apocalyptically in the latter stages of his ministry in order for them to have made the connection to Scriptures and especially to John's preaching just a few years before. I think Ehrman has it right when he writes in a later book that "some of Jesus's followers came to think that Jesus was raised from the dead. This changed everything for them" (Ehrman, 2004, p. 91).

As I will mention again in Chapter 7, all three of my major sources agree that Jesus' ministry was initiated by his association with that of John the Baptist. According to Funk, most of the Jesus Seminar scholars went further. They felt that "Jesus accepted what John was up to and thereby belonged to the movement initiated by him," but they "also affirmed that at some point Jesus deliberately separated himself from John's movement" (Mark 1:14; John 3:22–24) (Funk et al., 1998, pp. 54–55).

In my view, it is clear that the likelier scenario, if indeed Jesus' emphasis regarding the coming of the kingdom did change, is that it changed from apocalyptic to non-apocalyptic, not the other way around. I think it unlikely that Jesus' understanding of God's will (much less, God's will itself) changed twice, first away from apocalyptic prophesying—such as John had engaged in—and then back to it. And since I believe that God caused the post-crucifixion appearances of Jesus, I consider it likelier that if God did lead Jesus to change his message, then Jesus did not, because of that change, make a prophecy that turned out to be incorrect—a prophecy of an imminent end of the age—but rather taught the message that God wanted reconciliation with sinners.

Here is what I think may have happened. Jesus did begin his ministry as a protégé of John the Baptist; he may well have prophesied along the lines of Mark 13.

At some time, either gradually or suddenly, he began to sense that God wanted him to provide a different message. His focus became the in-breaking of a relationship with God that would develop over time as women and men came to understand both God's limitless love for them and God's will that they enjoy life's blessings and share those blessings generously with others. Jesus might have seen himself as helping to implement a prophecy of Jeremiah.

In Jeremiah's understanding of God's will, he records God speaking of a new covenant for Israel: "'It will not be like the covenant that I made with their ancestors when I took them by the hand to bring them out of the land of Egypt—a covenant that they broke, though I was their husband [or *master*],' says the LORD. 'But this is the covenant that I will make with the house of Israel after those days,' declares the LORD: 'I will put my law within them, and I will write it on their hearts; and I will be their God, and they shall be my people'" (Jeremiah 31:32–33).

At some point in his ministry, he began describing God's new relationship as the "kingdom of God" (or "imperial rule," as used by the Jesus Seminar, or some such name), but what he came to envision was not like the kingdoms of the secular world. In at least the later stages of his ministry, Jesus was describing a familial relationship, as is so well symbolized by his calling God *Abba*, the Aramaic word for one's daddy (Perrin, 1974, p. 281; Funk et al., 1997, p. 149). Law written upon minds characterizes kingdoms of this world; law written upon hearts characterizes a smoothly-functioning family.

When he went to Jerusalem, his confrontational behavior, including the disruption he created at the temple, got him into trouble with the temple priests, who saw their already limited theocratic control under attack. Pontius Pilate, anxious to keep any sort of unrest from escalating, was willing to go along with the priests' demand for Jesus to be executed. Possibly the talk of some sort of a new kingdom that might oppose Rome made his decision easier.

After the crucifixion, Jesus' followers sought some way to deal with what their society would deem Jesus' shameful, humiliating death. But after his appearances, the answer was—or rather, seemed—obvious. It is possible that Jesus himself had predicted his resurrection in his ministry, but in any case, the followers—some probably recalling prophecies from the book of Daniel in the Jewish Bible, the non-canonical book of Enoch, the teachings of John the Baptist, and maybe the early teachings of Jesus—took the appearances to be the sign of the end of the world as we know it. The sermon on the day of Pentecost that Luke attributes to Peter in Acts 2 may be at least a reasonable facsimile of what Jesus' disciples began to proclaim.

Paul, a few years later, picked up on that emphasis, and the rest, as they say, is history … except that when Matthew and Luke wrote their gospels, many of the later teachings of Jesus—which, although they were not included in Mark's gospel, had been preserved in oral or written form—were added into the gospel framework introduced by Mark. Those gospel writers toned down the apocalyptic fervor of much of Mark's gospel to better coincide with their additions to Mark's framework, and they attributed non-apocalyptic post-resurrection sayings to Jesus near the very ends of their gospels. (I'll have more to say about those "closing statements" in Chapter 7.)

This is all pure conjecture, of course, but I think it is nearer to what happened than the other alternative, if indeed Jesus did change his message.

I feel comfortable with the possibility that both the apocalyptic tone of the early Christian movement as represented by Mark, and the non-apocalyptic additions to Mark's gospel by Matthew and Luke, are faithful to Jesus' teachings. But I also see a big difference between the messages the two types of writings convey regarding how we should respond to his teachings. In one, we are to act out of fear of punishment and hope of reward, as if we were employees in a business run by a strict taskmaster; whereas in the other, we are to act out of heartfelt compassion, as members of a family led by a loving parent.

Conclusion and Looking Ahead

Jesus taught mostly about the kingdom of God, and based on considerable research, Perrin was convinced that Jesus used the "kingdom of God" not as a *sign*, but as a *symbol.* The difference, as Perrin used those terms, is that if it was used as a *sign*—that is, something pointing to a specific thing, such as a particular event—then preachers' responsibility should be "earnestly to look for signs of the end and busily to calculate dates for the coming of the Son of Man." If, however, Jesus used it as a true *symbol*—something that evokes thoughtful response—then preachers' responsibility should be "to explore the manifold ways in which the experience of God can become an existential reality to people" (Perrin, 2003, p. 33). I agree with his conclusion, at least as it applies to the later stages of Jesus' teachings.

In Part 2 of this book, I explain my conviction that the alleged post-resurrection appearances really happened—and that they were God's doing. Then, in the third part, I will discuss my view that, at least by the time his earthly ministry was coming to an end, Jesus looked forward to a gradual development of a kingdom of God on earth, in which the reality of God is experienced in heartfelt compassion for all God's creatures. I will also discuss what I believe this conclusion implies for today's world.

PART 2:

The Alleged Post-Crucifixion Appearances

3

Four Facts Related to the Claims of Post-Crucifixion Appearances of Jesus

Much of the debate about the supposed resurrection of Jesus has focused on the events allegedly surrounding the resurrection itself: Had Jesus been buried in a tomb? If so, on that Sunday morning did the women go to the right tomb? If appearances did occur, why are there such differences between the gospel accounts of them? These are all valid questions, but without new evidence, scholars are probably not going to be able to arrive at answers upon which they can all agree.

We can, however, use some statements widely accepted as facts to come up with circumstantial evidence concerning the fundamental question of whether the alleged appearances occurred. These statements concern the crucifixion itself and what happened in the months and years following the crucifixion. Here they are.

1. Jesus of Nazareth was in fact crucified by the Romans at the instigation of the Jewish authorities in Jerusalem at some time in the early thirties CE. He had had good reason to expect that outcome.

2. Shortly after the crucifixion, some of those who had been his closest followers began to preach—often at some risk to their lives—that God had raised Jesus from the dead and that Jesus would soon return in power to save those who believed in him.

3. In spite of continued persecutions by both Roman and Jewish authorities, the Christian movement grew steadily through the first century of its existence.

4. Paul, a contemporary of Jesus, did in fact write several of the letters ascribed to him in the New Testament, including Romans, 1 and 2

Corinthians, Galatians, Philippians, and 1 Thessalonians.

This chapter explores the evidence for these four statements, with considerable help from sources mentioned earlier. I need, however, to emphasize first that *the goal of this procedure is not to prove anything*. What I will claim is that, for me, the likeliest explanation of the evidence presented is that the four statements are true.

1. *Jesus of Nazareth was in fact crucified by the Romans at the instigation of the Jewish authorities in Jerusalem at some time in the early thirties CE. He had had good reason to expect that outcome.*

It is reasonable to believe, on the basis of both the New Testament and non-Christian sources, that Jesus was a real person and that he was crucified under the administration of Pontius Pilate, the Roman prelate of Judea at the time.

The Roman historian Tacitus, writing in *Annals*. xv.44, stated that "the founder of this sect, Christus, was given the death penalty … by the procurator Pontius Pilate …." Tacitus probably used information coming indirectly from Christians, but at least "[h]e tells us in effect that Roman historians accepted as factual …

that the founder of the Christian movement had been crucified by Pontius Pilate (Perrin, 1974, p. 283).

A passage in the "Babylonian Talmud" from "the first or second centuries" reads: "On the eve of Passover they hanged Yeshu [of Nazareth] and the herald went before him forty days saying, '[Yeshu of Nazareth] is going forth to be stoned in that he hath practiced sorcery and beguiled and led astray Israel. Let everyone knowing ought in his defense come and plead for him.' But they found naught in his defense and hanged him on the eve of Passover" (Perrin, 1974, pp. 283–284).

This passage disagrees in several details with the New Testament accounts of the crucifixion, but it does indicate Jewish assent, fairly early on, to the idea that Yeshu (Jesus) was executed. Moreover, the reference to pleading in his defense implies that it was believed he was first provided "a formal trial before Jewish authorities" (Perrin, 1974, pp. 283–284). As stated in my old college textbook, "The common element about Jesus found in both Roman and Jewish tradition is that he was a crucified false-teacher" (Beck, 1954, p. 72).

Jesus probably expected to be severely criticized and quite possibly crucified. He had come to Jerusalem, the seat of Israel's religious authority and power, just before Passover, one of the times when the Roman troops and authorities would be on heightened alert in Jerusalem. (Pontius Pilate did not normally stay in Jerusalem but would come, accompanied by extra soldiers, when religious celebrations in Jerusalem might be the source of uprisings against Roman authority.) Jesus could have anticipated a plot by the religious authorities to have him killed, because he would continue his attack on the kind of business that Judaism had become.

Moreover, it is likely (Perrin, 1974, p. 288; Funk et al., 1997, pp. 329–330) that Jesus had said something like the words in Luke 11:20: "But if it is by the finger of God that I cast out the demons, then the kingdom of God has come to you." (Ehrman notes that this verse is not in Mark (Ehrman, 1999, p. 130). It is essentially stated in Matthew 12:27–28, however, and therefore the Jesus Seminar concluded that it came from Q, that separate source used by Matthew and Luke.) Such statements, suggesting a special relationship between God and an "outsider" such as Jesus, would have been seen by the temple authorities as heretical and would have led to the charge that Jesus had "practiced sorcery and beguiled and led astray Israel." The religious authorities did not have the power to have persons executed, but the Roman authorities did, and anyone threatening to disrupt the peace of the city in that tense time would be a likely prospect. That is why the timing of Jesus' arrival—on "the eve of Passover"—is significant.

2. *Shortly after the crucifixion, some of those who had been his closest followers began to preach—often at some risk to their lives—that God had raised Jesus from the dead and that Jesus would soon return in power to save those who believed in him.*

That the Christian movement was initially led by some of the apostles is also implied by Paul, who refers in Galatians 2:9 to coming to an agreement with "those reputed pillars of our society, James (identified in Galatians 1:19 as "the Lord's brother"), Cephas (Peter), and John."

From the outset, the belief that galvanized the movement and served as the claim upon which non-Christians were asked to put their faith in Jesus as Savior was that Jesus had been brought back from the dead and that those who believed in Jesus would likewise be resurrected.

Paul's first letter to the Christians in Corinth states that "if there is no resurrection of the dead, then Christ has not been raised; and if Christ has not been raised, then our proclamation has been in vain and your faith has been in vain. We are even found to be misrepresenting God, because we testified of God that he raised Christ—whom he did not raise if it is true that the dead are not raised (1 Corinthians 15:13–15).

One reason that preaching the resurrection was so important is that Judaic Scripture had never associated the "suffering servant" concept with the concept of a messiah. Harris points out that "[n]o passage in the Hebrew Bible even hinted that the Messiah would die, let alone be executed as a felon by Gentile agents" (Harris, 2000, p. 439). Jews would thus initially take the fact of Jesus' crucifixion as solid evidence that he was *not* the awaited Messiah, as Ehrman has noted (Ehrman, 2000, p. 54). Focusing on the resurrection helped to overrule that perception.

The belief in Jesus' coming back soon as a judge seemed a natural extension—given belief in Jesus' resurrection—of the apocalyptic writings in the book of Daniel that at the end of the world as we know it, many will rise from the dead to receive their just rewards or punishments. In addition, John the Baptist was an apocalyptic prophet, whether or not Jesus himself was. According to Matthew, John had warned his audience, "Even now the ax is lying at the root of the trees; every tree therefore that does not bear good fruit is cut down and thrown into the fire" (Matthew 3:10).

If Jesus had risen, the logic would have gone, the end time must have begun. And Jesus—he who was the first to rise and thus "the one who has inaugurated the beginning of the end"—was God's chosen one and "was soon to return in judgment on the earth" (Ehrman, 2000, p. 53). These conclusions certainly occurred to the ex-Pharisee Paul, who, in what is believed to be the earliest portion of the New Testament, wrote of Jesus as the one "who rescues us from the wrath that is coming" (1 Thessalonians 1:10).

A number of the early leaders of Christianity were killed by either Roman or Judaic authorities. Historians believe that James the son of Zebedee was executed by the order of Herod Agrippa I, as reported in Acts 12:1–3, and that this occurred no later than 41–44 CE (Harris, 2000, p. 556). The first-century Jewish historian Josephus wrote that in the early sixties a high priest ordered the execution of James, Jesus' brother or half-brother (Harris, 2000, p. 504), who, after the crucifixion, had become one of the leaders of the Christians in Jerusalem. Many scholars believe that Paul was martyred in Rome, probably in 64 or 65 under Nero's reign, and that Peter probably was also (Perrin, 1974, p. 199; Harris, 2000, pp. 574, 575).

3. *In spite of continued persecutions by both Roman and Jewish authorities, the Christian movement grew steadily through the first century of its existence.*

There is no evidence of any substantial lapse during the first century in the activity of the Christian movement. Scholars generally agree that the letters truly written by Paul date from the fifties. Writing in the *HarperCollins Study Bible*, Ronald F. Hock included the following passage in regard to Philippians 2:6–2:11: "These verses, as their format shows, are widely regarded as a pre-Pauline Christ hymn; Paul's letters frequently contain material from earlier Christian tradition (e.g., Romans 1:3–4, 3:24–25; 1 Corinthians 15:3–5; 1 Thessalonians 1:9–10)" (Meeks, 1993, p. 2205). The Synoptic Gospels and John were probably written in the period extending roughly from 70 to 100 CE.

External sources of information about the spread of the Christian movement usually refer to the troubles Christians were having with non-Christians. Writing around 120, the Roman historian Suetonius reported that the emperor Claudius "expelled from Rome the Jews who were constantly rioting at the instigation of a certain Chrestus" (Perrin, 1974, p. 283). Although "Chrestus" might refer to someone other than Jesus, it is probably an alternate spelling of the word "Christus" used by Tacitus. And Christians' speaking of Christ as being with them probably explains why Suetonius seemed to have thought that the instigator was physically present. More likely than not, this passage refers to the expulsion noted in Acts 18:2. The date of that event is not known precisely, but Claudius' reign ended in 54 (Beck, 1954, p. 70).

In about 115, the Roman historian Tacitus claimed that Nero used Christians as scapegoats for the great fire in Rome in 64, and consequently that "Nero had self-acknowledged Christians arrested. Then, on their information large numbers of others were condemned—not so much for incendiarism as for their anti-social tendencies. Their deaths were made farcical. Dressed in wild animals' skins, they were torn to pieces by dogs, or crucified, or made into torches to be ignited after dark as substitutes for daylight … Despite their guilt as Christians, and the ruthless punishment it deserved, the victims were pitied. For it was felt that they were being sacrificed to one man's brutality rather than to the national interest" (Tacitus, *Annals* 15.44, as cited in Harris, 2000, p. 430).

As I suggested earlier, Tacitus' information was "probably based on the police interrogation of Christians and so is not actually independent of the

New Testament or the Christian tradition" (Perrin, 1974, p. 283). However, the mere fact that he, an upper-class intellectual, felt that Christians deserved ruthless punishment suggests that they were looked upon with scorn in first-century Rome (Harris, 2000, p. 430) and adds credibility to the assertion that self-acknowledged Christians were in fact being severely persecuted in Rome in about 64.

Writing at roughly the same time as Tacitus, Pliny the Younger, a Roman governor in what is now Turkey, wrote to the Roman Emperor Trajan regarding questions of how to deal with persons who admitted being, or were accused of being, Christians.

> I do not know the nature or the extent of the punishments usually meted out to [Christians] ... Nor am I at all sure whether ... a pardon ought to be granted to anyone retracting his beliefs, ... and whether it is the mere name of Christian which is punishable, even if innocent of crime, or rather the crimes associated with the name.
>
> For the moment this is the line I have taken with all persons brought before me on the charge of being Christians. I have asked them in person if they are Christians, and if they

> admit it, I repeat the question a second and third time, with a warning of the punishment awaiting them. If they persist, I order them to be led away for execution; for, whatever the nature of their admission, I am convinced that their stubbornness and unshakeable obstinacy ought not to go unpunished … I have entered [the names of "similarly fanatical" Roman citizens] on the list of persons to be sent to Rome for trial.…
>
> … [A] great many individuals of every age and class, both men and women, are being brought to trial, and this is likely to continue. It is not only the towns, but villages and rural districts too which are infected through contact with this wretched cult. (Kaegi, W. E. and P. W. White, eds., 1986, pp. 260–261)

These passages attest not only to the persecution of early Christians but also to the steady spread of the Christian movement in its first century. And of course the New Testament book of Acts independently attests to both the persecution and the constancy of the spread as well.

Ehrman has written about the causes of all this persecution. In *Forged*, he notes that there was no official Roman condemnation or persecution of Christians "in its first two hundred years," but their refusal to participate in sacrifices intended to keep the many Roman deities happy caused much concern. It is understandable that when things went wrong, Christians often were blamed. Moreover, their habit of meeting in private homes and in secret (presumably due, at least in part, to the hostility they encountered) led to all sorts of rumors about licentiousness and extremely immoral behavior taking place at their meetings. And the Jews, of course, discouraged the spread of what they considered to be a ridiculous but dangerous spinoff from traditional Jewish practices and beliefs (Ehrman, 2011, pp. 164–167).

4. *Paul, a contemporary of Jesus, did in fact write several of the letters ascribed to him in the New Testament, including Romans, 1 and 2 Corinthians, Galatians, Philippians, and 1 Thessalonians.*

Most scholars doubt the claim that all the books (letters, really) ascribed to Paul in the New Testament were actually written by him, but his authorship of the five mentioned here is not generally contested. I will use quotations from these letters later.

The relevance of these four facts will be discussed in the next chapter.

4

The Four Facts Considered, in Regard to the Alleged Appearances

It has often been stated that something spectacular must have happened to the disciples to cause them to begin to spread, at great risk to their lives, the message that Jesus was Lord and Savior. This chapter develops that conclusion, based on the conclusions given in Chapter 1 and the four facts discussed over the course of Chapter 3, namely:

1. Jesus of Nazareth was in fact crucified by the Romans at the instigation of the Jewish authorities in Jerusalem at some time in the early thirties CE. He had had good reason to expect that outcome.

2. Shortly after the crucifixion, some of those who had been his closest followers began to preach—often at some risk to their lives—that God had raised Jesus from the dead and that Jesus would soon return in power to save those who believed in him.

3. In spite of continued persecutions by both Roman and Jewish authorities, the Christian movement grew steadily through the first century of its existence.

4. Paul, a contemporary of Jesus, did in fact write several of the letters ascribed to him in the New Testament, including Romans, 1 and 2 Corinthians, Galatians, Philippians, and 1 Thessalonians.

As in Chapter 3, I am not attempting here to prove anything, but I shall argue that, for me, the likeliest explanation of the four facts is that some sorts of appearances of Jesus after the crucifixion were instigated by God. To avoid unnecessary verbiage, I will hereafter refer to the alleged post-crucifixion appearances as simply "appearances."

So, what is the likeliest explanation of the curious combination of what I will now call "facts" number one through four above? Specifically, why did those early followers of Jesus—to be joined in a few years by Paul—begin to preach Jesus' resurrection, given the opposition that they faced? The short answer seems clearly to be: because of the appearances.

There are several ways in which the accounts of the appearances might be completely baseless as evidence of "divine intervention." The appearances may not have occurred at all, the early leaders of the movement having just fabricated stories about appearances; or the appearances may have been hoaxes, perpetrated to fool the disciples or perpetrated by the disciples to fool others; or they may have been hallucinations in which disciples' minds fooled them into believing a falsehood. The following subsections discuss these possibilities.

The Possibility That They Made It All Up

Suppose first that some of the disciples conspired to make up stories about appearances, in order, perhaps, to symbolize the continuing presence of Jesus in their hearts, similar to the way some people interpret the resurrection in modern times. It is difficult to see why the accounts of the appearances would differ so much if they were fabricated as part of a plan. Another issue is whether it is reasonable to attribute to his first followers both the devising of such a plan and, especially, the ability to carry it out successfully. But the biggest question I have here is: *why* would they have made up the accounts?

It is, of course, true, according to Mark's gospel in passages copied by Matthew and Luke, that Jesus had told his closest followers three times that he must die and rise again. But there is no evidence in those gospels that, if Jesus had in fact made that prophecy, the disciples began to believe it until that following Sunday. There is nothing in the Synoptic Gospels that suggests that, up until then, the disciples had expected or even hoped for a resurrection. In other words, according to all three Synoptic Gospels, fact number two implies a drastic change in what had been the disciples' mind-set: a change from depression, foreboding, and, quite possibly, fear, to exultation and courage. There had to be a cause for that change.

If, at the beginning of the Christian movement, those early leaders did not firmly believe that God had in some sense brought Jesus back to appear before them, what motivation would they have had to devote themselves to spreading that proclamation—knowing that they would face persecution that quite possibly could end in their being executed, as Jesus had been?

If they had known or even suspected that God had *not* in some sense produced appearances of Jesus, I think it highly unlikely that they would have been the least bit interested in the small possibility of acquiring, very possibly at the cost of their lives, some degree of fame as the founders of a probably short-lived movement. Common sense would dictate against that path.

More importantly, *even if they had believed beforehand that a resurrection would occur*, would they not have needed some hard evidence *after* the crucifixion that Jesus was not just deluding himself, or them at least, in speaking of his coming resurrection or of the end of the world as we know it? They might have wanted to believe that the end of the age was upon them, but where was a confirming sign? Their leader had been killed, and their lives were already at risk for having been his followers. *Why not*, they must have felt, *just wait and see if the end comes? Why stick our necks out any farther? Why not lie low until we see some confirmation?*

If Jesus had prophesied in the manner of Mark 13—if the disciples were thinking apocalyptically at all—they would surely have waited for signs of the end to begin so that they could point to them as corroboration that the world was ending. In fact, they do seem to have waited only a very short time before feeling that corroboration *was* at hand. Apparently the appearances of Jesus provided the corroboration they sought.

The Possibility That They Were Tricked or Intended to Trick Others

Next, suppose that the early leaders of the movement were tricked, either by Jesus himself or by others, into believing that Jesus had appeared after his crucifixion. Some have conjectured that his crucifixion may not have been fatal. Death by crucifixion has in some cases required many more hours than Jesus is thought to have suffered on the cross. (The episode recorded as Mark 15:44–45 was probably added at some point in the gospel's history as an effort to counter or preclude speculation about that possibility. Its authenticity, however, is doubtful, inasmuch as it would represent probably unrecorded communications between Roman authorities.) In that case, Jesus himself, perhaps disguised in some way to prevent immediate recognition, could have instigated so-called "appearances."

Problems with this hypothesis include the question of why the Roman guards, presumably good at their jobs, would have released his body without being sure he was dead. Even to be accused of having made such an error would most likely have caused them to be executed.

Moreover, the idea of Jesus deliberately setting up the disciples to live and die for a lie is so out of character with what Jesus taught as to be unbelievable. Why, moreover, would he have so disrespected the God he called his Father?

Alternatively, a look-alike impostor could have been brought in, either by a disciple or to trick the disciples. Who would have done that, and for what purpose? If it was to fool the disciples, certainly neither the Roman nor the Jewish authorities would have done it except to set a trap, and no such trap seems to ever have been sprung.

Moreover, the possibility of some sort of hoax having been perpetrated—by Jesus himself or an impostor, by whatever means—is made less likely by "fact" number three. One would expect a hoax to stand little chance of going undiscovered over a long period of time, if it served as the basis for a movement opposed by both Jewish leaders, who considered it heretical, and Roman authorities, who saw it as disruptive and disloyal to the emperor. Moreover, had even some solid indication of a hoax been discovered, it would surely have been trumpeted as clear proof of the false basis of Christianity throughout the region. If even a hint of such a hoax had circulated, first-century Christians would have defected in droves from their newly found faith. Why would one take a chance on a belief that might well be false, when that belief might easily bring persecution and even death? And yet the growth of the new faith seems to have been steady.

It is of course possible that a hoax was discovered, or at least widely suspected, and that all references to it in the records kept in Roman circles were expunged in the time of Constantine, who made Christianity an acceptable religion in the Empire. However, such scant evidence as I am aware of on either side of this question points in the opposite direction. The letter by Pliny the Younger, from which a quotation was given in Chapter 3, indicates that there were some self-proclaimed Christians who recanted upon the threat of death, but it makes no mention of any decrease in the numbers of self-designated Christians due to any other cause. In fact, the "infection" had spread to "not only the towns, but villages and rural districts too" (Kaegi, W. E. and P. W. White, eds., 1986, pp. 260–261).

Paul's stay in Jerusalem (described in Galatians 1) three years after his conversion also adds weight to the assumption that no significant claim of a hoax was circulating in the first few years after the crucifixion, since in his letters Paul never saw a need to discount such a claim.

Also, word of a suspected hoax would presumably have reached Jewish authorities, and there would be no reason for any Jewish records of a possible hoax to have been sealed away or destroyed.

That leaves an evaluation of the likelihood that each of the appearances was some sort of hallucination. I will use that word *hallucination* in a nontechnical way to mean "a perception, while in the conscious state, in the absence of an external material stimulus and in the absence of direct involvement by God." A technical definition recently given by T. M. Luhrmann, in work to be considered below, omits the reference to God (Luhrmann, 2012, p. 216).

The Possibility That They Were Hallucinating: Lapide's Views

Pinchas Lapide—a Jewish rabbi and theologian whose belief that Jesus was in fact resurrected is described in *The Resurrection of Jesus: A Jewish Perspective*—wrote that "most Jewish scholars" consider as the likeliest explanation of the resurrection reports the possibility that they rested on "visions of individual persons" stemming from their own powers of imagination. "It could have been a case of honest autosuggestion—as we find it now and then in the Talmud. Disciples see their departed master in a dream. A whole table fellowship believes strongly in Elijah, sees him present, and speaks with him. Where the power of faith is involved, Jews have a power of imagination that sometimes borders on the supernatural—without any need to doubt the subjective honesty of that which is experienced" (Lapide, 1982, p. 124).

Lapide himself would not accept that answer. "No vision or hallucination is sufficient to explain such a revolutionary transformation" as occurred in the lives of Jesus' disciples (Lapide, 1982, p. 125). After quoting several different scholars' understanding of what "the resurrection of Jesus" really means, he wrote: "Most of these and similar conceptions strike me as all too abstract and scholarly to explain the fact that the solid hillbillies from Galilee, who, for the very real reason of the crucifixion of their master, were saddened to death, were changed within a short period of time into a jubilant community of believers. Such a post-Easter change, which was no less real than sudden and unexpected, certainly needed a concrete foundation which can by no means exclude the possibility of any physical resurrection" (Lapide, 1982, pp. 129–130).

The Possibility That They Were Hallucinating: Lüdemann's Views and My Responses

On the other hand, in *The Resurrection of Christ: A Historical Inquiry*, Gerd Lüdemann, a New Testament scholar at the University of Göttingen, provides a strong defense of the possibility that the appearances were all generated completely in the brains of the disciples.

Before responding to Lüdemann's view, I will point out an important difference in his goal and mine. His purpose is to give a convincing attack on the thesis that Jesus was bodily resurrected: "If Jesus' resurrection did not take place and consequently Jesus was not revived and changed into a divine being, then [no ways of justifying the Christian faith] can help. In that case Christian faith is as dead as Jesus and can be kept alive only by self-deception" (Lüdemann, 2004, p. 19).

My purpose will be to give what is for me a convincing argument that at least some of the reported appearances were the result of God's direct intervention in some way—whether by resurrection of the human body, resurrection in a spiritual body, a supernaturally caused revelatory vision, or by some other way, I don't know. In each of at least three or four cases, I think the reported appearance can be characterized as, in Lüdemann's words, "a spiritual experience unlimited by the protocols of the time-space world or subject-object relationships" (Lüdemann, 2004, p. 47), with the addition that the appearance was caused by God.

A large portion of Lüdemann's book deals both with what happened to Jesus' body and the many different accounts of appearances of Jesus after his crucifixion. He notes the ambiguities and contradictions and the fact that many facets of the accounts could well be the work of a later generation of Christians. My focus is on the appearances only—and only certain appearances, at that.

At this point, I need to discuss what Paul, in what is probably the oldest source of reports, wrote in regard to early appearances: "For I handed on to you as of first importance what I in turn had received: … that [Christ] appeared to Cephas, then to the twelve. Then he appeared to more than five hundred brothers and sisters at one time, most of whom are still alive, though some have died. Then he appeared to James [Jesus' brother or possibly half-brother], then to all the apostles" (1 Corinthians 15:5–7).

It is appropriate here to restate fact number four from Chapter 3: Paul did in fact write several of the letters ascribed to him in the New Testament, including Romans, 1 and 2 Corinthians, Galatians, and Philippians. In other words, we have in those letters some original source material, written—almost certainly prior to any of the New Testament's gospels—by a person intelligent enough and articulate enough to write letters such as those addressed to the Romans and the Galatians. (We do not have the original letters, but I think it is unlikely that later scribes or editors would have altered what Paul considered a key affirmation as to what he had heard and believed to be true.) Moreover, it is reasonable to assume that Paul, a well-educated Pharisee, was aware of the power of "honest autosuggestion," which, according to Lapide, is characteristic of Jews "where the power of faith is involved." Paul's letter to the Galatians mentions that he had zealously studied "the traditions of [his] ancestors" (Galatians 1:16). And in the passage quoted above, Lapide noted that autosuggestion is evident in the Talmud, which was composed some centuries later but included ancient folklore.

In what follows, I will consider the words ascribed to Paul in the genuine Pauline letters to be the most reliable source of information about the appearances.

Peter's Vision

Lüdemann's fourth chapter is entitled "The Faith of the Early Christians in Jesus' Resurrection: Origin and

History of a Self-Deception." Here he focuses first on the appearance to Peter. Citing cases of hallucinations of departed loved ones and recent investigations of causes of inhibited or unsuccessful mourning of widows and widowers, Lüdemann concludes that Peter's experience "is an example of unsuccessful mourning" in which "the unconscious is unable to bear the loss of a beloved person and creates artificial fulfillments for itself" (Lüdemann, 2004, p. 165). He goes on to cite a Harvard study of factors "inhibiting or preventing a successful passage through the mourning period: first, a sudden death; second, an ambivalent attitude toward the deceased, involving feelings of guilt; and third, a dependent relationship." A recent article notes that in fact most adults grieving the loss of their mates "acknowledge having [at some time] heard, seen, or otherwise sensed their departed partners" (Bower, 2012, p. 23).

One obvious question is whether these studies have a lot to say about Peter's emotions and the workings of his unconscious during the time between Jesus' crucifixion and the appearance to Peter.

That time interval was probably short. It seems likely that the disciples were still in or near Jerusalem when Peter experienced the appearance to him alone. Matthew took literally Mark's account of Jesus' saying that he would meet his disciples "in Galilee" (Mark 14:28). Perrin considered the use of "Galilee" in Mark's gospel to be a symbolic reference to the Gentile world (Perrin, 1974, pp. 150–151), much as the terms "Main Street" and "Wall Street" are currently used to distinguish between the features of two American subcultures. Lapide indicates that "Galilee" may instead have referred originally to an area near Jerusalem (Lapide, 1982, pp. 113–114). But even if Peter did experience Jesus' appearance in Galilee, the time interval for grieving would not have been long. Examples drawn from persons having a difficult time in *completing the mourning process*—having trouble making a "successful passage" through it—don't seem to me to apply very strongly to a person whose grief had begun only a short time beforehand.

In any case Lüdemann's approach seems to require the assumption that Peter's most prominent emotion in those days immediately following the crucifixion was grief, accompanied by ambivalence about Jesus, guilt, and a sense of dependence. That may, of course, be correct. However, my impression of Peter leads me in different directions, mostly.

Peter was, of course, grieving Jesus' death. His relationship to Jesus, however, was primarily that of a follower to a charismatic leader. This leader's decisions had not only led to his own execution; they had also put his followers in grave danger. *Why*, they must have wondered, *had he come to Jerusalem at this dangerous time and acted the way he had?* This is a radically different circumstance from that of someone grieving for a lost spouse or child. Peter's situation would, in my view, elicit ambivalence, yes, but more bewilderment than deep-seated grief. Prominent among Peter's emotions, I think, were also fear (Would the authorities come looking for Jesus' disciples?) and shame for having been disloyal at the most critical time. I'm not sure that he felt guilt. It doesn't seem likely to me that he would have felt responsible for the death of Jesus. Nor do I envision Peter as having a strong sense of dependence on Jesus, as he could always return to the life of a fisherman.

Another issue concerns how imaginative Peter and, for that matter, all of "the Twelve" were, considering their apparent inability, prior to the appearances, to get beyond the Hebrew Bible's image of a military Messiah who would free Israel from foreign domination. Nonpsychotic hallucinations have recently been studied intensively by Stanford anthropologist T. M. Luhrmann, who notes that they depend on the capacity to consider what one imagines as more real than one's physical surroundings (Luhrmann, 2012, pp. 194–202, 243).

How strong was this capacity in Peter? Even if, as Luke's gospel asserts, he had heard a report that the tomb was empty and that Jesus had risen, was Peter's unconscious strong enough to produce, soon after the crucifixion, a comforting image of Jesus that his conscious mind could accept as more real than sensory data? It is possible, but I see very little similarity between this possibility and the hallucinations of parents or spouses working through their grief. Viewed from our knowledge that Peter was an early leader of the Christian church, it is easy to suppose that, to relieve his troubled mind, his unconscious might have constructed a non-threatening apparition of the person he might soon be allowed to serve. But in fact he had little, if any, reason to believe, consciously or unconsciously, that there could possibly be any movement in which he might serve. As Lüdemann put it: "Peter's world had collapsed" (Lüdemann, 2004, p.163).

How likely would it be that his unconscious, in trying to provide some "artificial fulfillment," would be able to convince Peter that Jesus would still love him after his ultimate disloyalty? I would think that if in those dark days Peter's unconscious had wanted to give him some relief, it would have chosen a safer route, perhaps having Peter imagine as more real than his physical surroundings a comforting voice from heaven, maybe accompanied by a mental picture of a fishing boat—but *not* accompanied by an image of the man he had deserted in the time of greatest need.

I favor the possibility that, in some manner not covered by the laws of nature, God presented Jesus to Peter in a revelatory vision or in some other way—and in a manner that communicated that Jesus did indeed still love him and wanted to work with him.

That this simpler answer is not considered by Lüdemann is not surprising. An article in *Newsweek* in 1996 attributed to Lüdemann the opinion that "the Resurrection is an 'empty formula' that must be rejected by anyone holding a 'scientific world view'" (Woodward, 1996, p. 62). As I discussed in Chapter 1, science cannot, by its very nature, rule out the possibility of divine intervention in the affairs of this world. To claim that it can is scientism, not science.

The Visions of Other Original Disciples

For Lüdemann, the alleged appearances to the other original disciples were in essence caused by Peter's experience, and therefore "the discovery of the origin of the faith in Jesus' resurrection is really the quest for the origin and nature of [Peter's and Paul's] transformational experiences" (Lüdemann, 2004, pp. 153–154). I will keep to the probable chronological order and discuss the appearances to the other disciples and to Jesus' brother James before turning to Paul's case.

"Not long after Good Friday," Lüdemann writes, "Peter experienced a vision that included auditory features, and this event led to an extraordinary chain reaction … Peter experienced Jesus' appearance to him as reacceptance by the one whom he had repudiated; the other disciples experienced it as forgiveness for their desertion" (Lüdemann, 2004, pp. 173, 174). Thus it was that "[t]he first vision of Peter proved formally infectious, and was reportedly followed by others—one to the Twelve, and another to more than five hundred at one time" (Lüdemann, 2004, p. 175). In bolstering these claims, he cites philosopher Ernest Renan's view that "in an assembly of persons entertaining the same beliefs, it is enough for one member of the society to affirm that he sees or hears something supernatural, and the others will also see and hear it" (Renan, as quoted by Lüdemann, 2004, p. 175).

I admit that such a chain reaction would be possible even for those "solid hillbillies from Galilee" as Lapide called them; and if it did happen, I definitely agree with Lüdemann that it was an extraordinary event. In any case, although I trust Paul's report of having been told that appearances had been made to "the Twelve" and to "five hundred brothers and sisters" (1 Corinthians 15:5–6), and I trust that Paul believed those assertions to be based on fact, I don't see any way to add to the defense of their accuracy.

James' Vision

According to the information Paul received on a visit to Jerusalem, Jesus had appeared to James the son of Mary (1 Corinthians 15:7). This James was not mentioned in the Synoptic Gospels as a disciple prior to the crucifixion. According to the earliest Synoptic Gospel, Jesus' "mother and his brothers" wanted in fact to curtail his ministry (Mark 3:21, 31–32). But there is strong evidence that he became actively involved in the early Christian movement. "Among those who [claimed to have seen Jesus alive], interestingly enough, was Jesus' own brother James, who came to believe in Jesus and soon after became one of the principal leaders of the early Christian church" (Ehrman, 1999, p. 229).

Lüdemann understands the appearance to James as an effect of the "dynamic power" of the movement based on earlier appearances, a power "so compelling that the natural brothers of Jesus were caught up in the excitement, and went to Jerusalem. James even received an individual vision—the same James who had little to do with his brother during Jesus' lifetime, and seems to have participated in the [family's] attempt to have his 'crazy' brother put away" (Lüdemann, 2004, pp. 175–76).

This scenario could be exactly what happened, but I think it misrepresents, somewhat, both the context in which the early Christian movement operated and what James' turnabout must have been like for him. Surely from its beginning the movement faced vigorous opposition from the authorities. To those who had not been following Jesus before, joining the movement must have seemed a seriously dangerous, foolhardy move. And Lüdemann's approach trivializes, in my opinion, the distress through which James must have gone in deciding to make such a drastic change in his life. As Lüdemann suggests, James had probably not been neutral regarding Jesus' ministry; he most likely had opposed it.

To me, an appearance of Jesus engineered by God seems to be much more likely as the cause of James' conversion than a hallucination. Luhrmann's research led her to a pattern that typically describes nonpathological hallucinations, one characteristic being that they generally do not cause distress (Luhrmann, 2012, p. 243). This conclusion is reinforced by the modern-day accounts Lüdemann provides in support of his evaluation of Peter's experience (Lüdemann, 2004, pp. 163–165). If James' unconscious had wanted to soothe inner turmoil, it would likely have presented the message that it was all right to stick with the original family position in regard to Jesus. Even though some people were *claiming* that Jesus had risen, no painful, embarrassing turnaround would be required; and furthermore, there would be no need to put oneself in mortal danger.

The Jesus Seminar expresses doubt about the appearance to James. It "seems to be an attempt to put James on an equal footing with Peter (and perhaps Paul)" (Funk et al., 1998, p. 455). But I wonder what—other than an appearance—could have caused such a reversal in James' life.

Moreover, on an early visit to Jerusalem, Paul had lodged with Cephas (Peter) for fifteen days. He had also seen James, "the Lord's brother" (Galatians 1:18–20). Thus by his own account Paul had had the opportunity to question these two men about what they themselves had experienced. Obviously, whatever he heard from them satisfied Paul that the appearances to

Peter and James were both God's doing, not some sort of honest autosuggestion. He calls the information he received on this visit to Jerusalem "of first importance" (1 Corinthians 15:3) as independent evidence in support of the claim he was about to make: that Jesus had appeared also to him. He viewed the appearances prior to his conversion and the appearance to him as two mutually supporting verifications that God was actively at work in the establishment of the Christian movement. In this context, I trust that Paul not only heard that James had seen Christ but also had ample reason to believe it.

Paul's Vision

As in the case of Peter's resurrection appearance, Lüdemann ascribes Paul's Damascus road experience entirely to forces at play in Paul's unconscious. In Paul's letters (and especially in Romans 7), Lüdemann sees evidence of "conflicting emotions" that were "too loaded with experience" not to have been present in Paul's unconscious mind before the appearance on the Damascus road. In particular, Lüdemann suggests that Paul must have been struggling with the implicit assault, by the teachings of Jesus and some contemporaries, on Paul's understanding of God as "a wrathful deity". He also suggests that Paul was probably struggling with the concept of a crucified Messiah. Finally, Lüdemann proposes that Paul may have been unconsciously attracted to the possibility of becoming the "Apostle-in-Chief of a new program of salvation with a culture-wide appeal" (Lüdemann, 2004, pp. 170–171). I have some doubts regarding these conjectures. They all provide possible reasons for whatever it was that Paul experienced, but do they add up to the implication that the appearance was most likely a hallucination?

There may well have been turmoil in Paul's mind, focused on a conflict between the Pharisaic and the Christian doctrines of God, or whether a crucified person could actually be the Messiah, or both. If he had begun to doubt whether he had been right in persecuting the Christians, he would have been wrestling with the difficulties he would face in completely turning his life around. As in the case of James, a non-distressful hallucination intended to alleviate those inner struggles would have had the message that no drastic turnaround was required: he had not been wrong. If, on the other hand, Paul was "blindsided" by the appearance, inner turmoil would have had no role to play in its origination.

I question the likelihood of Lüdemann's third suggested motivation. Viewed from our knowledge of the steady rise of Christianity in its first century, it is easy to suppose that Paul might unconsciously have wanted to lead a "culture-wide" program toward its ultimate triumph over the Pharisees (even though Paul was himself a Pharisee). However, having been a persecutor of the movement himself, he must have been aware that in its first years Christianity was under attack: it did not enjoy a culture-wide appeal, and it might well have been crushed in its first decade. Caiaphas, the high priest when Jesus was tried, remained in power until at least 36; and, as mentioned earlier, the "other James" (the son of Zebedee) is thought to have been executed no later than 41–44.

As Paul made clear in the first sentence of his letter to the Galatians, he saw his mission and his ministry as not in any way derived from or dependent upon the testimony of the first leaders of the Christian movement. Moreover, as mentioned earlier, he was most likely aware that he could have experienced an appearance that was not of divine origin. And yet he was so convinced of the authenticity of his experience of Jesus' presence that he too devoted the rest of his life to spreading the good news that "God was in Christ, reconciling the world to himself" (2 Corinthians 5:19). Scholars think he died, probably by execution, in a Roman prison. Was he either deceiving himself or suffering from a mental illness?

Apparently the members of the congregations he helped to establish didn't think so; I don't think so, either.

I am not claiming that Jesus was necessarily present in a physical body on the Damascus road. Acts 9:7 states that the men with Paul "saw no one." It is, however, clear to me that—given the conclusions defended in Chapter 1—the likeliest explanation of Paul's Damascus road experience is that, as Paul himself surely believed, it was God's doing, perhaps in the sense of "a supernatural appearance that conveys a revelation," to quote a definition of *vision* given by *Webster's New Collegiate Dictionary*. Presumably, Paul would have said that the resurrected Christ he experienced was in a spiritual body, since he referred to Christ as the firstfruits of the resurrection, and to resurrected bodies as spiritual bodies (1 Corinthians 15:20, 44).

I am not a psychologist and my efforts to psychoanalyze first-century Judeans are no more than uninformed opinions. And I have certainly not done the massive amount of research that Lüdemann used as the basis for his conclusions. He is a New Testament scholar; I am not. But to me, the hypotheses that the appearances to Peter and Paul originated in unconscious efforts to calm troubled minds, and that the appearance to Jesus' brother was somehow due to his being caught up in the excitement, are poorly supported by the circumstances, as I understand them to have been. Based on my view that science cannot rule out divine intervention, I think that the simpler explanation that those appearances were God's doing is much likelier.

Other Possible Interventions

If God provided such an event (vision or not) to convert one who could and did play a major role in the spread of the Christian faith to the Gentile world, it is reasonable to assume that God—as necessary—would have acted in other, similar ways in order to get the Christian faith started and to keep it growing in its first few years. Both Peter and Paul apparently saw clear evidence of God's hand at work in their own work of spreading the Christian movement. Paul undoubtedly saw God's support in his surviving floggings, a stoning, three shipwrecks, and numerous imprisonments (2 Corinthians 11:23–27); and I would be surprised if there were no kernel of truth in the account in Acts 3 of Peter curing, in Christ's name, a man's lameness.

It also seems likely to me that both sons of Zebedee—James, who was killed on order of Herod Agrippa I, and John, whom Paul considered a pillar of the movement—would have needed reinforcement of their initial experience of a post-crucifixion appearance in order to have continued to promote the Christian faith as they did, if they even suspected that that first encounter might have been due to Peter's powers of persuasion, as Lüdemann proposes.

Some Christian or Christians other than Paul carried the movement to Rome. Would carrying the faith to the heart of the Roman Empire have been attempted solely on the basis of an appearance that could have been explained away in some manner? Citing Renan, Lüdemann notes that the people of the Judaic culture believed not only in miracles but also in phantoms (Lüdemann, 2004, p. 175). An account in Luke of an appearance of Jesus to the disciples includes the description that at first the disciples "were startled and terrified, and thought that they were seeing a ghost" (Luke 24:37). Whether or not that passage is historically accurate, the report itself corroborates Renan's claim that, in that culture, belief in phantoms and ghosts was widespread. It seems to me that when one or more disciples started the work of establishing a Christian community in Rome, they would have been greatly tempted to opt out of their leadership roles when the dangers started to mount, because they could easily have convinced themselves that what they had originally seen had *not* been provided by God, but was instead just a ghost of the man Jesus. Under those circumstances, would God not have provided them with additional evidence of support? Again, I think God did whatever was needed in those early days to get the movement going and to keep it growing.

Lapide would, I think, agree. As noted earlier, he thought the results of the appearances provide strong evidence in favor of their being authentically God's work. Citing the famous rabbi Maimonides in support of his opinion, Lapide held that "[t]he experience of the resurrection as the foundation act of the church which has carried the faith in the God of Israel into the whole Western world must belong to God's plan of [worldwide] salvation." Lapide referred to Judaism and Christianity as hoping for "a common messianic goal" (Lapide, 1982, pp. 142, 153).

The Jesus Seminar considered the appearance of Christ to Peter as probably reliable (coded pink) and Christ's appearance to Paul as reliable (coded red) (Funk et al., 1998, pp. 453–454). In addition, the Jesus Seminar scholars "felt obligated to acknowledge the claim of Mary [of Magdala] to have had a vision of the risen Jesus," and they coded red the affirmation that she "was among the early witnesses to the resurrection of Jesus" (Funk et al., 1998, pp. 478–479).

What about those alleged appearances to women, found in various forms in Matthew, Luke, and John but not mentioned by Paul? It seems unlikely that such allegations would have been fabricated, given the low esteem in which most men held women in that culture. In my view, appearances of some sort did occur. Given my belief that God engineered appearances to Peter, James, and Paul, I think the likeliest conclusion to draw is that the appearances to the women—or, following the Jesus Seminar, at least to Mary the Magdalene—were God's doing also. Surely they deserved to receive such a confirmation, if, as the gospels report, they did not desert Jesus at his crucifixion. Very possibly Paul might not have been told about those appearances, or he may not have considered them as reliable evidence of God's direct action. His views on the status of women seem to have been fairly typical for Jews of his day.

I do agree with one major theme of Lüdemann's book—namely that the four gospels most likely include some materials that embellish and quite possibly contradict what would be included in a historically correct report of the events occurring immediately after Jesus' crucifixion. But I also respect Paul's integrity and intelligence, both in regard to his evaluation of what he learned about the appearances to Peter and James, and in regard to his evaluation of his own conversion experience. Based on my confidence in those conclusions, I am confident that God had Jesus appear also to Mary the Magdalene, even though Paul does not mention it.

Other Opinions, Other Doubts

Other Opinions

I am aware that some leading twentieth-century theologians, including Rudolf Bultmann, considered the accounts of appearances to comprise a "myth" in the theological sense of that term. In that sense, a *myth* is a story that points to truths that cannot be fully captured in historical events or even fully grasped by the finite human mind. Unlike Dietrich Bonhoeffer, who considered the resurrection as "unlike all myths" (Hordern, 1968, p. 223), Bultmann held that the biblical accounts of appearances do not describe actual events but instead point to the reality of the "spiritual presence of Jesus" in the profession of the Christian faith. Thus "Bultmann boldly asserts that for him Jesus is risen—into the [proclamation] of the church" (Perrin, 1974, p. 22).

I accept that some of the church's proclamation—such as the claim that Jesus now "sits at the right hand of God"—seems to have the character of religious myth in the theological sense that I mentioned. I am convinced, however, that at least some of those first Christians must have experienced something God did, or the movement would never have gotten off the ground. Perrin considered the appearance to Paul to have been a revelatory "vision of a figure who identified himself as Jesus of Nazareth" (Perrin, 1974, p. 94). In my opinion, the appearances to Peter, James, and Mary were also of that nature.

Other Reasons to Doubt

Gentiles were accustomed to stories about resurrection appearances, many after three days' time. Lapide's book surprised me with the following statements: "[I]n the ancient world there were not less than a round dozen of nature deities who, all long before Jesus, [were said to have] suffered, died, and rose again on the third day … Some died on the cross. The death of some deities even had expiatory power … [I]t had to appear to many contemporaries of the early church that the story of Jesus is basically no more than another mythology of a father of gods who lets his son die and raises him back to life to save his believers" (Lapide, 1982, pp. 40–42).

Does this fact weaken the argument that the appearances of Jesus were God's doing? Lapide thought not. In a later chapter, he pointed out the difficulty of persons in basing their faith on a concept completely foreign to their previous experience, and he suggested that God patterned the appearances after those ancient myths to make the appearances conceivable to the Gentiles (Lapide, 1982, p. 122). This brings to mind the account in Acts of a sermon Paul delivered in Athens. According to this account, Paul found an altar with the inscription "To an unknown god." He skillfully used that opening to introduce his audience to "[t]the God who made the world and everything in it" and who "does not live in shrines made by human hands" (Acts 17:24).

An aspect of the story of Jesus' appearances that probably helped to set it apart from those ancient mythologies was the belief on the part of many in the early church that, as Jesus went to the cross, he was himself neither God nor a Son of God at birth.

Very near to the beginning of Paul's letter to the Romans, he described the gospel message this way: "The gospel concerning his Son, who was descended from David according to the flesh and was declared to be Son of God with power according to the spirit of holiness by resurrection from the dead, Jesus Christ our Lord" (Romans 1:3–4). Scholars think this passage is probably part of an early confession of faith, since it does not represent what Paul himself seems to have believed (Meeks, 1993, p. 2116). According to Harris, "[T]he oldest layer of preserved tradition suggests that the first Christians saw Jesus, like Israel's anointed kings, becoming God's Son by adoption, a reward conferred at his resurrection and ascension to heaven" (Harris, 2000, p. 431). Ehrman, referring to early Christians holding such beliefs as adoptionists, notes that "adoptionistic Christologies can be traced to sources that predate the books of the New Testament" (Ehrmann, 1993, p. 48).

A reason that many persons doubt the reality of the appearances is that they seem to have been witnessed by only those who had been followers of Jesus, except for the cases of Paul and probably Jesus' brother James. Why, many wonder, did not everyone, including the leaders of the temple and the Romans, witness the events? Lapide provides a clue in words quoted from Eduard Schweizer: "God exposes himself to skepticism, doubt, and disbelief, renouncing anything that would compel men to believe" (Schweizer, as quoted in Lapide, 1982, pp. 118–119). In *The Secret Message of*

Jesus, McLaren elaborates this point. "As soon as the evidence [of the resurrection] becomes irrefutable, it takes on a kind of domineering power—the kind of force so effectively wielded by principalities and [worldly] powers" (McLaren, 2006, p. 71).

As I will discuss in a later chapter, I believe, as does McLaren, that God wants a kingdom that does not operate through that kind of power. I believe that instead, God seeks a kingdom on earth that works on compassionate love. God wants us to love our neighbors as ourselves, not because that is a commandment and we had better obey it, but instead because it will just come naturally—because we, like God, will have hearts of compassionate love.

Conclusion

Taking into account the conclusion I drew in Chapter 1, I believe that the likeliest explanation of at least some of the alleged appearances is that they were, in some way, God's direct intervention. *Could* all of the appearances either have resulted from some other cause or not have happened at all? Of course. But I don't believe it.

5

Possible Reasons for the Appearances, in My View

In this short chapter I will set the stage for addressing what I think were the main purposes of the appearances of Jesus, again in the context of my belief that those appearances were made possible by God's direct action. From here on, I do not claim to be applying a facts-based method. The chapter titles imply that these are just my current opinions, and they are very much influenced by my personal background and experiences through life. I freely acknowledge that, from here on out, all of my views may be wrong. Some of them may be partially right. All I claim is that they are what I currently believe.

An imminent end of the world had been predicted by John the Baptist and, quite possibly at some time, by Jesus himself. Instead, there was a crucifixion followed by the appearances—but no end of the age. Why not? Why did God allow Jesus to be crucified? And why, as I believe, did some of Jesus' disciples and Paul experience Jesus in some meaningful ways *after* the crucifixion? What impact or impacts were intended? Surely, as one reason for the appearances, God wanted to glorify Jesus for his willingness to die on the cross in service to God's kingdom. But there may well be other reasons for the appearances. If so, what might they be?

Jesus may have predicted the destruction of the Jerusalem temple—or possibly Jerusalem itself—as indicated in Mark 13:1–2, and the appearances could have been provided to herald the culmination of that prediction. The temple was destroyed in 70. However, there is no evidence that that prediction was a major part of Jesus' message, if he did in fact make it.

The possible reason for the appearances most likely to have been on the minds of the earliest Christians is that the appearances heralded the end of the age, since—whether or not Jesus had predicted it—they felt that Jesus was about to return. That did not occur, at least in the fashion that they had anticipated, and the fact of its nonoccurrence presented a problem for the advancement of the Christian faith in the decades that followed.

As many now believe, God may have led Jesus to prophesy about events that would affect the entire world but would not occur for many generations, and then caused the appearances in part as a testimonial supporting the fact that those events would occur *someday*. Thus the apocalyptic discourse in Mark 13 is widely taken to describe an end of the age, which will yet come. After all, verse 30, which reads, "Truly I tell you, this generation will not pass away until all these things have taken place," may not be original with Jesus.

On the other hand, in the time of the prophets whose messages are described in the Hebrew Bible, the purpose of prophecies inspired by the Holy Spirit was to try to change behavior for the better in the *near, foreseeable* future. The story of Jonah may not be based on historical events, but in any case, the message attributed to Jonah epitomizes the role of the biblical prophets: "Forty days more, and Nineveh shall be overthrown!" (Jonah 3:4).

I think Jesus' prophecies, if he made any, would most likely have concerned the generation to whom he spoke and perhaps the next generation. That is, I think Jesus most likely would himself have thought that he was predicting events in the relatively near future. Vindicating a prediction of an *imminent* end of the age was clearly not a motivation for the appearances. Nowadays, cartoons sometimes feature strange-looking persons carrying signs that read something such as "The end is near!" Of course, it may in fact be near, and Christ may soon be seen coming from heaven, as many believe. My point is that a prophecy whose fulfillment has been delayed for nearly two thousand years is not an obvious asset to the doctrines of a faith, nor would one expect it to be very effective in determining how most persons live their lives.

I therefore don't think that the appearances were meant to support an apocalyptic prophecy. If they had been, the apocalypse would have happened long before now. This conclusion is reinforced by my belief that, at any particular time, the future is truly open. I do not think that God knew in the first century what life on this planet would be like in the twenty-first century. (I myself consider the Spirit of Christ, living in and guiding the Holy Spirit, to be in human hearts here and now—in the words of a familiar carol, "where meek souls will receive Him still, the dear Christ enters in.")

It likewise seems clear to me that God did not intend to vindicate, to those generations, any prophecy Jesus might have made or implied about an imminent social revolution in which the saying "the last will be first, and first will be last" (Matthew 20:16) would apply literally to living conditions in this world. Within about forty years of the appearances, there was indeed social upheaval in Israel, but it was not of the type that could be said to have vindicated a call for social revolution. Matters had remained bad in Israel and then worsened, culminating in the destruction of the temple, mentioned above. Thus the possibility of God wanting to vindicate a prediction of a positive social restructuring of first-century Judea is also eliminated, in my view.

I see three possible, mutually compatible reasons, beyond the desire to honor Jesus, for God to have chosen to engineer the post-crucifixion appearances. These three candidates are "functional" in the sense of having to do with positive, lasting impacts on the world of the first century and beyond. Taken together, they clearly outweigh the cost of the appearances—that is, the confusion that the appearances caused in regard to the anticipation of a cataclysmic end of the age that did not happen.

First, they may have been meant in part to confirm the accuracy of the image of God that came from Jesus' teachings about God and God's kingdom. In Chapter 7

I will address what I think the focus of those teachings was.

Second, the appearances set the stage for a Jesus-based movement to spread beyond Israel. I touched on this idea near the end of Chapter 4 in connection with the resurrection stories prevalent at that time in pagan cultures.

And third, they set the stage for a new first step toward full participation in the kingdom of God proclaimed by Jesus—namely the truth that, as Paul wrote, "[i]f you confess with your lips that Jesus is Lord and believe in your heart that God raised him from the dead, you will be saved. For one believes with the heart and so is justified, and one confesses with the mouth and so is saved" (Romans 10:9–10).

Implicit in these statements are Paul's views that Jesus' crucifixion paid the penalty for the sins of those who accept him as their Lord (believers are justified by grace through faith in Christ), and that Jesus' resurrection proved that believers would also be resurrected and saved, rescued "from the wrath that is coming" (1 Thessalonians 1:10). The next chapter discusses this good news – this "gospel" – of Paul.

PART 3:

The Implications for Us, in My View

6

My View of Jesus' Message in Relation to Paul's Gospel

We all fashion our religious beliefs or nonbelief in large part on our life experiences, and I think that Paul was no exception. I am not aware of any evidence that Paul at any time studied the oral traditions that were later incorporated into the Synoptic Gospels, the stories about what Jesus had said and had done before the crucifixion. On the other hand, he had been a Pharisee (Philippians 3:5), which gave him not only a thorough knowledge of the laws attributed to Moses, but also a strong inclination to see righteousness (being reconciled to God) in terms of "justification"—being pronounced or declared righteous. Thus, Paul, citing Genesis 15:6, noted that Abraham believed God and "it was reckoned to him as righteousness" (Galatians 3:6).

Also, his Damascus road experience convinced him that Jesus was the first of the persons who—according to Old Testament prophecy—would be resurrected at the end of the world as we know it. This belief drove Paul, who was undoubtedly guided in his work by the Holy Spirit, to conceive of reconciliation with God primarily in terms of obtaining *the promise of salvation*, which he thought would be granted very soon for all those who qualified for it.

Recognizing that we humans cannot free ourselves from sinful behavior, Paul based his conception of salvation on the grace—the undeserved love—of God for humanity. Salvation is God's gift, which is provided to all who put their faith in Jesus to save them and who believe that God raised Jesus from the dead, thereby confirming Jesus' lordship and the possibility of resurrection (Romans 10:9–10).

The basis for the now-traditional concepts of a two-story abode for eternity, a blissful heaven and a fiery hell, is found in the book of Daniel, which was written in the second century before Christ, and in some apocryphal writings from roughly the same time. Since Jesus, and later Paul, presumably used the concept of eternal punishment in hell without explanation, it seems clear that it was a concept generally understood by the rank and file of Jewish people in that time.

Under the combination of all those circumstances, it is very understandable that Paul began to preach that we can be justified before God and thereby saved from eternal retribution in the fires of hell, if we believe Jesus to have been raised and accept the risen Christ as our Lord and Savior. Thus in his first letter that we have, he wrote that "the day of the Lord will come like a thief in the night" and that, although some persons will be suddenly destroyed, "God has destined us not for wrath but for obtaining salvation through our Lord Jesus Christ" (1 Thessalonians 5:2–3, 9). In what is considered Paul's most refined account of his theology, he was still emphasizing salvation by justification: "Much more surely, then, now that we have been justified by his blood, will we be saved through him from the wrath of God" (Romans 5:9). To Paul, then, the gospel, the good news, was "the power of God for salvation to all who have faith" (Romans 1:16).

I see this as the message God wanted Paul to proclaim. Therefore, it represents an important new thing that God has done. It is not only different from the route to reconciliation with God as described by a number of prophets in the Hebrew Bible; it is also different from the message Jesus himself gave about the way to restore a right relationship with God. After all, according to the Synoptic Gospels, Jesus' message was focused on the in-breaking of the kingdom of God, not on Jesus himself. On the other hand, I do not believe the primary purpose of the appearances to have been solely to lay the groundwork for the announcement of this new thing. My explanation of this position requires the rest of this chapter.

Comparison of the Concepts of Reconciliation and Salvation

Famous passages from the Hebrew prophets stress that the path to reconciliation with God requires correcting relationships with others and especially with those others who have little wealth or power.

Speaking of God, Micah proclaimed, "He has told you, O mortal, what is good; and what does the Lord require of you but to do justice, and to love kindness, and to walk humbly with your God?" (Micah 6:8).

Speaking as God might, Amos said, "Therefore because you trample on the poor and take from them levies of grain, you have built houses of hewn stone, but you shall not live in them; you have planted pleasant vineyards, but you shall not drink their wine … Take away from me the noise of your songs; I will not listen to the melody of your harps. But let justice roll down like waters, and righteousness like an ever-flowing stream" (Amos 5:11, 23–24).

Isaiah said, "Your new moons and your appointed festivals my soul hates; they have become a burden to me, I am weary of bearing them … Wash yourselves; make yourselves clean; remove the evil of your doings from before my eyes; cease to do evil, learn to do good; seek justice, rescue the oppressed, defend the orphan, plead for the widow" (Isaiah 1:14, 16–17).

According to a preponderance of material in the Synoptic Gospels, Jesus taught that, for a person to be forgiven of sin, two things were required: the forgiving of those who had sinned against that person, and the asking of a gracious God for forgiveness—with the firm intention of not repeating the sin, the cause of estrangement from God. (That second step is often implicit in Jesus' words, since the Judaic society believed in God's willingness to forgive a "contrite heart.") Thus, participation in God's kingdom, which requires reconciliation with God, begins with a willingness to forgive others and a heartfelt desire to be forgiven. "And forgive us our debts as we also have forgiven our debtors" (Matthew 6:10).

There is support for this claim from several portions of the gospels that are generally considered to authentically represent what Jesus said or might have said. Ehrman calls the importance of forgiveness "one of the most widely attested teachings of Jesus" (Ehrman, 1999, p. 173). Examples include the parable of the unforgiving servant (Matthew 18:23–34), the story of a servant who, although his own debt was forgiven, refused to forgive the debt that another person owed to him. His punishment was to be tortured until he had repaid every bit of the debt for which he himself had been forgiven. Although it is often taken as an allegory, taking it just as a story Jesus probably told about humans interacting with each other suggests the importance Jesus seems to have given to forgiving one another.

The most concise support of my claim is Luke 6:37c, which has Jesus saying, "Forgive, and you will be forgiven." Ehrman cites the verse as an example of what Jesus taught (Ehrman, 1999, p. 174), and the Jesus Seminar scholars agree, coding it pink—meaning that "Jesus probably said something like this" (Funk et al., 1997, pp. 296–97). I agree, and I consider it to be a crucial part of Jesus' concept of the kingdom of God—a first step into that kingdom.

As previously indicated, Paul, on the other hand, seems to have come at the concept of reconciliation as primarily a relationship between a person and God, a reconciliation requiring acceptance of the lordship of Christ in one's life and belief in the truth of the resurrection. Although, in his letters to fellow Christians, Paul frequently did urge his readers to be kind and respectful in interacting with each other, the concern expressed in the Hebrew Bible's Torah for how the stranger, the alien, was to be treated is less in evidence in those letters. Understandably, Paul's principal concern seems to have been the health of the Christian movement: he did not want the movement to be damaged or held back by fractious behaviors among its members. In his letter to the Galatians, he did identify what might be considered general "fruit of the Spirit": "love, joy, peace, patience, kindness, generosity, faithfulness, gentleness, and self-control" (Galatians 5:22). Not very many lines later, however, he wrote, "whenever we have an opportunity, let us work for the good of all, and especially for those in the family of faith" (Galatians 6:10).

In *A New Kind of Christianity*, Brian McLaren sees this concern of Paul at the heart of Paul's thinking. McLaren confronts the question of how, in the light of what Jesus seems to have emphasized, we are to understand Paul's theology, "especially [in] that pivotal letter, Romans." McLaren argues that "Paul wasn't trying to define or explain the gospel at all; rather he was trying to clean up a mess that Jesus had created through his gospel." He explains that Jesus had, by example, sanctioned the disregarding of traditional categories, boundaries, and rules associated with the Judaism of his time; and Paul, in his letter to the Romans, was "simultaneously defending the right of the gentile Christians to be different and struggling to keep Jews and Gentiles working together as one community." That is, Paul was primarily seeking to hold together the early Christian community, people who had accepted Christ as Lord and who believed in his resurrection, consisting as it did of persons with or without Jewish backgrounds. "I became convinced," McLaren writes, "that Paul never intended his letter to be an exposition on the gospel" (McLaren, 2010, pp. 142–43). This view, which McLaren supports with a discussion of the book of Romans, seems plausible to me.

It seems to me that Paul's prescription of sincere confession and belief provides an alternative way to *enter* God's earthly kingdom, without focusing on how to participate in the activity of that kingdom—the latter being a key part of what Jesus talked about.

Entry into God's kingdom implies reconciliation with God. As I have admitted, there may be literal truth contained in the vision of a day of judgment as presented in the book of Daniel, a time in which some of us will awake to eternal life and some "to shame and everlasting contempt" (Daniel 12:2). If, as Jesus may have believed and as Paul must have believed, there is a place of eternal bliss for those who are accepted by God, surely heartfelt belief in Jesus as the risen Lord and Savior will suffice to get us there. And if, as Jesus may have believed and as Paul must have believed, there is a place of everlasting contempt and eternal torture, then surely that same belief will save us from that place.

But I do not believe that any of Paul's writings should be taken as superseding Jesus' own teachings about becoming reconciled with God. After all, for people to confess that Jesus is Lord of their lives *should* imply that they try to follow Jesus' teaching as best they can. Paul expressed faith in Christ in terms of acquiring a relationship to God through which a person is deemed "righteous," reconciled to God. Such a relationship must, I think, be in accordance with the key features of the message Jesus taught by word and by deed. Thus, in my opinion, those who truly and fully forgive the persons who have wronged them, or try their best to do so, will not be subjected to punishment in the next life if they ask God for forgiveness.

In any case, I think that *Jesus' own gospel is much wider and richer than the Pauline gospel*, because forgiving others, the "original" first step toward full participation in the kingdom of God, is just a first step. My view is that Jesus himself was primarily concerned with the good news that God wants to fully reconcile the world—*this* world, and all of it—to God's self, not in terms of being declared justified (righteous), but by continually striving to live as Jesus taught us to live.

I believe that God wanted Paul to help the Christian movement to grow into something more than a (probably short-lived) Jewish sect. Paul was presumably not very familiar with Jesus' teachings, and in any case, those teachings would not have won over many converts among the polytheists he met in his missionary journeys. And Ehrman is, I think, probably correct in conjecturing that if, in the first decades after Jesus' crucifixion, the message of his followers had not been based on the post-resurrection appearances, the movement would never have been extended to the Gentile world. Paul taught that "[s]alvation did not come by the Law, but by the death and Resurrection of Jesus. This notion of salvation, apart from the Law, was a notion that Paul developed, more than anyone else, and without this notion being developed, Christianity would have remained simply a sect of Judaism. It would not have become a separate religion, because Jesus's own preaching wasn't about his death and Resurrection, overcoming sin and death. His preaching was about the coming Kingdom of God" (Ehrman, 2004, p. 85).

Ehrman suggests, more or less, the following as the line of thought that Paul may have taken: (1) Since he had seen Jesus after the crucifixion, Jesus must be in some sense alive; (2) therefore Jesus' death on the cross must have special meaning, because a man good enough to be raised from the dead did not deserve to die on the cross in the first place; and so (3) it must be that Jesus was supposed to be crucified for some special reason. (4) The easiest answer as to why he was supposed to die on the cross was that he died not to pay the penalty for his own sins—which, if there were any, would certainly not be deserving of crucifixion—but to pay for the sins of humanity (Ehrman, 2004, pp. 82–83).

And that answer seems logical. After all, must not a *just* God *require* a penalty for sin? I now need to explain my personal view of God's concept—or rather, *concepts*—of justice.

Concepts of Jesus

In the perspective summarized by "Forgive, and you will be forgiven," God is seen as a God of justice, primarily in the sense of seeking just and loving relationships among all persons, both individually and collectively. This kind of justice, based on God's unlimited love for all persons everywhere, would be a key characteristic of the kingdom of God, fully come to earth.

As noted earlier, there *are*, of course, passages in the gospels that attribute to Jesus words to the effect that God is a vengeful God, and consequently, that if people do not change their ways (to *repent* meaning "to turn around or turn back"), they will suffer in hell. A prime example is in Mark, our oldest gospel.

> If any of you put a stumbling block before one of these little ones who believe in me, it would be better for you if a great millstone were hung around your neck and you were thrown into the sea. If your hand causes you to stumble, cut it off; it is better for you to enter life maimed than to have two hands and to go to hell, to

> the unquenchable fire. And if your foot causes you to stumble, cut it off; it is better for you to enter life lame than to have two feet and to be thrown into hell. And if your eye causes you to stumble, tear it out; it is better for you to enter the kingdom of God with one eye than to have two eyes and to be thrown into hell, where their worm never dies and the fire is never quenched. (Mark 9:42–48)

Ehrman uses verses 47 and 48 to illustrate Jesus' warning of the destruction that the coming of the kingdom will bring (Ehrman, 1999, p.154). That may be a correct interpretation, especially if this saying came early in his ministry. There is, however, a different interpretation:

Jesus may have been emphasizing the importance of getting one's heart right with God, as opposed to simply following a set of specific rules, which, after all, can never cover all possible ways in which sinful behavior can occur. In so doing, Jesus may have used the apocalyptic images of hell and hellfire metaphorically as a helpful tool for getting his point across, as they were symbols that could easily have been familiar to his hearers. The *HarperCollins Study Bible* notes that "[u] ndying *worm* and unquenchable *fire* are stock images for the destruction of evil" (Meeks, 1993, p. 1936), citing as one example the final verse in the book of Isaiah.

Similarly, in *The Secret Message of Jesus*, McLaren quotes Dallas Willard's observation that, by carrying the Pharisees' emphasis on following the law to its logical conclusion, Jesus may have wanted to shake them out of their mind-set so they might realize what was really important: compassionate love (McLaren, 2006, p. 124). The Jesus Seminar scholars, in spite of their tendency to disregard passages using apocalyptic imagery, colored Mark 9:43–47 gray, signifying the opinion that "Jesus did not say this, but the ideas contained in it are close to his own." Funk and Hoover report that some of the Jesus Seminar fellows felt that the imagery "could echo the voice of Jesus," noting the similarity between the image of tearing out one's eye to those verses in the Sermon on the Mount (Matthew 5:29–30), which call leering at a woman tantamount to adultery (Funk et al., 1997, p. 86).

In these views, Mark 9:42–48 is not a prophecy of the destruction of evildoers by a wrathful God but an attention-getting way of describing what is *not* present in the kingdom of God.

A number of other passages in the gospels ascribe to Jesus words that describe God as a God of vengeance, of retribution. In some of those cases as well, it is possible that Jesus was just using apocalyptic imagery to emphasize God's displeasure with behavior that tends to curtail participation in the kingdom.

In his little book, *Love, Power, and Justice*, Paul Tillich, a leading twentieth-century theologian, described different "levels" of justice, and claimed that "retributive" justice seems not to have been at the level on which Jesus focused his attention. Tillich notes three general forms of justice, the first of which is an intrinsic claim based on the power of being, of existing. He calls the second form "tributive or proportional justice," which comes in three types. "Attributive justice attributes to beings what they are and can claim to be [as in attributing humanity to all races of human beings]. Distributive justice gives to any being the proportion of goods which is due to him; retributive justice does the same, but … in terms of deprivation of goods or active punishment. … In the realm of law and law-enforcement the tributive form of justice is the norm. But there are some exceptions, and they point to a third form of justice. I suggest that this third form be called transforming or creative justice" (Tillich, 1960, p. 64).

Creative justice is based on the "ultimate intrinsic claim for justice in a being," namely "[f]ulfillment within the unity of universal fulfillment. The religious symbol for this is the kingdom of God." Tillich adds that "[t]he classical expression of this third form of justice is given in the biblical literature of both Testaments" (Tillich, 1960, p. 65).

As I understand it, Tillich's concept of creative justice is based on the conviction that God loves us all, everywhere, the same—regardless of the circumstances that have contributed to the development of the kinds of persons that we individually have become. Those circumstances do not completely determine our character or our actions. We do have free will as we decide how to respond to the circumstances we face.

But at the same time, it is clear that many persons all over the world are born into conditions that provide little chance of enjoying opportunities for much self-determination in their lives. I believe that God wants those of us who have wealth and power, relative to those who have little to none of either one, to work for a world that is not unjust in this regard. Significant progress toward such a world is likely to require some considerable sacrifice on the part of wealthy, powerful societies. Moreover, as important as charity is, societal structures need to be rededicated to the pursuit of creative justice as much as is feasible. And that entails political action.

Taking action for the poor and needy worldwide is not the only implication of God's universal love, of course. Creative justice is put into action countless times every day and in every land by loving family members, good friends, and good-hearted strangers—"good Samaritans." God's love and God's hopes extend to us as well as to the poorest and neediest.

As developed by Anselm, Canterbury's archbishop in the twelfth century, Paul's doctrine of Jesus' death as a substitution for the penalty required of sinners became a "predominant doctrine in Western Christianity" (Tillich, 1960, p. 14). However, Tillich saw that understanding justice as including that higher level of creative justice provided a way to represent the *core idea* behind Paul's concept of justification by grace through faith. "In [that paradox], as stated by Paul, the divine justice is manifest in the divine act which justifies him who is unjust. This, like every act of forgiveness, can only be understood through the idea of creative justice. And creative justice is the form of reuniting love" (Tillich, 1960, p. 66).

The core idea, for Tillich, was that "ultimately love must satisfy justice in order to be real love, and … justice must be elevated into unity with love in order to avoid the injustice of eternal destruction" (Tillich, 1960, p. 14). Creative justice fits those requirements.

My view is that, for Jesus, creative justice is the goal, and true forgiveness exemplifies it. However, I believe that he would admit that circumstances can and often do require the application of distributive or retributive justice in the short term. Jesus may himself have dealt out some retributive justice when he saw what was going on at the temple in Jerusalem. Vengeance, on the other hand, seems counterproductive to the establishment of creative justice. The only goal of retribution should be either correction or the protection of others. If, as the gospel of Mark describes it, Jesus overthrew tables and chairs and generally disrupted business as usual at the temple in Jerusalem, the purpose clearly was correction, not revenge. He was protesting the depths to which Judaism was being corrupted, out of the lure of financial gain.

That Jesus saw God as favoring creative justice over retributive justice is strongly suggested by verses in the Sermon on the Mount, particularly Matthew 5:39–42 and 44–45. Creative justice is presented in stark contrast to distributive justice in the parable of the laborers in the vineyard (Matthew 20:1–15). The employer said to the first group of those standing idle for lack of a job that he would pay them whatever was "right" or just (Matthew 20:4). Then, at the end of the working day, all laborers were paid the same amount, regardless of how long they had worked. Assuming that the purpose of this parable, as with most of them, is to have us compare the illustrated behavior with our own, then what is the message here? In the employer's compassion for those who could not find work all day long, there seems to be the message that creative justice is what God wishes to see in us, *even when it clearly seems unfair*, as it surely would have to those laborers who had worked the whole day.

The parable of the prodigal son (Luke 15:11–32) is a presentation of creative justice completely overwhelming any inclination toward retributive justice. The first part of the story ends this way. "Then the son said to him, 'Father, I have sinned against heaven and before you; I am no longer worthy to be called your son.' But the father said to his slaves, 'Quickly, bring out a robe—the best one—and put it on him; put a ring on his finger and sandals on his feet. And get the fatted calf and kill it, and let us eat and celebrate; for this son of mine was dead and is alive again; he was lost and is found!' And they began to celebrate" (Luke 15:21–24).

In the second part of the story, the other son expresses a strong feeling that he himself has not been duly appreciated by his father. In the father's mind, however, a celebration was absolutely necessary. "But we had to celebrate and rejoice, because this brother of yours was dead and has come to life; he was lost and has been found" (Luke 15:32).

In *The Scandalous Gospel of Jesus*, Gomes stated that "the claim of a God … more gracious, more generous, more hospitable than [are those who worship him] is at the core of what Jesus calls the good news …" (Gomes, 2007, p. 41). Personally, I have for years been unable to believe that God's love for each of us, so boundless while we are alive, could allow us to be punished eternally after we die. The love even of (good) human parents does not end when a child dies, nor does the love even of (good) human parents condone punishment for the sake of a payback.

This approach leads immediately to another question. If God does not require Jesus' sacrificial death as a penalty for the sins of humanity, then is there still some sense in which Jesus' crucifixion saves us? I think there is, and I have addressed my personal views on this topic in Appendix 1.

Conclusions

I do believe in the adequacy of Paul's prescribed way to escape hell, if hell exists—and to reach heaven, if heaven exists. However, I do not believe that the primary long-range purpose of the appearances was to proclaim a way in which Jesus' death could save people from the everlasting punishment that God would otherwise inflict upon them in retaliation for their sinful behavior. The argument I have given does not deny the possibility of that purpose; it simply speaks against it—again, in my personal view—as the main motivation for the appearances. As I wrote in the preface, I am trying to stay faithful to what Jesus taught, and I believe his teachings are best represented in the Synoptic Gospels, according to which Jesus focused his message not on himself but on the in-breaking of the kingdom of God on this planet and in this continuing age. I do not believe that Paul taught anything that supersedes what Jesus taught, nor do I believe that he intended to do so.

That brings me back to the full list in Chapter 5 of possibilities, as I see them, for the functional reasons for the appearances of Jesus after his crucifixion. Beyond the desire to honor Jesus for all time to come, the appearances were, I believe, primarily intended: (1) to show God's approval of what Jesus had taught about

God and God's kingdom, so that his followers would continue to believe in Jesus' teachings and bring others into commitment to follow them also; (2) to allow God's kingdom to spread beyond Israel; and (3) to initiate a first step toward full participation in the kingdom of God that Jesus had proclaimed.

In my mind, these possibilities are all closely interconnected. I think God arranged the post-crucifixion appearances in the hope that Israel would "see the light" and correct its ways once more, and also in the hope that a new movement based on Jesus would become that "light to the nations" about which Isaiah had prophesied centuries before. Correcting Israel's ways meant adopting the way to live that Jesus had taught, and the post-crucifixion appearances would both confirm Jesus' message for the Israelites and facilitate its spread beyond Israel. Being a light to the polytheistic Gentiles would require emphasizing to them the power of God as revealed in the appearances themselves.

Then, in order for this new religion to have a chance to spread, at least one person with the powerful kind of message Paul preached would be needed. Viewed as an aid to the expansion of the Christian movement into the Gentile world, the "new mode of entry" to the kingdom of God provided by Paul (and later emphasized in the gospel of John) was crucially important.

For our own time, the purpose of ratifying Jesus' teachings about God and God's will is, in my opinion, more important. In the next chapter, I deal with my view of that part, at least, of what Jesus taught that is most relevant to us today: the non-apocalyptic part.

7

What Jesus Taught by His Actions and Words, in My View

What Jesus Taught by His Actions, in My View

I need now to give a brief discussion of Jesus' deeds, as represented in the Synoptic Gospels, and what he may have meant for them to teach—before discussing my view of the main content of his teaching.

Chapter eleven of Ehrman's *Jesus: Apocalyptic Prophet of the New Millennium* discusses Jesus' "associates, deeds, and controversies" as reported in the gospels. The deeds are examined in the apocalyptic context that his previous chapters have developed, and he finds "a very nice confluence" between the sayings and the deeds (Ehrman, 1999, pp. 183–184). In my opinion, his overall case for Jesus being best understood as an apocalyptic prophet is, in fact, well-served by that chapter.

In *The Acts of Jesus: What Did Jesus Really Do?*, the scholars of the Jesus Seminar seem to be more conservative than Ehrman in the number of biblical accounts of Jesus' actions that can be trusted. Although some of the exclusions decided on by the Seminar seem pretty questionable to me, the reason for exercising considerable conservatism is, I believe, justified. After all, followers of Jesus might be expected to remember the parables Jesus told and the aphorisms he used, but narrative accounts of Jesus' deeds are formulated from the outset by others and could be expected to be more fluid, in the transmission from one person to the next, than intriguing stories about interesting characters and pithy one- or two-line responses to challenging questions. Moreover, it is to be expected that, in the gospel writers' job of fitting Jesus' sayings into an overall narrative of his ministry, the writers would readily adjust the accounts of what Jesus did to provide a readable framework for the things he is reported to have said.

Perhaps the best approach for my purposes is to focus on four general features of actions attributed to Jesus—on which Ehrman, the Jesus Seminar, and Perrin all seem to agree. More or less, in Perrin's words, they are:

1. [Jesus] was baptized by John the Baptist, and the beginning of his ministry was in some way linked with that of the Baptist.

2. Jesus was above all the one who proclaimed the Kingdom of God and who challenged his hearers to respond to the reality he was proclaiming.

3. [His] authority and effectiveness … as proclaimer of the Kingdom of God was reinforced by an apparently deserved reputation as an exorcist. [H]e was able, in the name of God and his Kingdom, to help those who believed themselves to be possessed by demons.

4. Low social status—as in being among the outcast—did not prevent anyone from full participation in his group of followers. Thus "Jesus challenged the tendency of the Jewish community of his day to fragment itself and in the name of God to reject certain of its own members." (Perrin, 1974, pp. 287–88)

In addition to these four features, Ehrman and, writing for the Seminar scholars, Funk agree with (in Funk's words) "the statement that Jesus performed some anti-temple act and spoke some word against the temple" (Ehrman, 1999, pp. 208–209, 211–214; Funk et al., 1998, p. 121). In the preceding chapter, I gave my opinion of what Jesus was trying to teach by the disturbance he apparently caused in the Jerusalem temple—namely, that the economic system that had developed around Judaism was corrupting the Judaic religion itself.

Item 1 deserves discussion in connection with the curious fact that in the Synoptic Gospels much material suggests that Jesus was an apocalyptic prophet following in the footsteps of John the Baptist; and yet much material suggests that he was not. I have dealt previously with the possibility that Jesus began as an apocalyptic prophet but changed his mind at some point in his ministry about what God wanted him to say about the kingdom. (It is, of course, possible that he changed his mind at the start and then later changed back to an apocalyptic message.)

Item 2 reflects the uniform opinion of my chief sources that the gospel of John, while serving as an invaluable source of inspiration and strength for Christians of all ages, was not intended to be biographical, even to the degree that characterizes the Synoptic Gospels. However, the emphasis in John's gospel on love—God's love for the chosen and the love they should have for one another—is similar to what I believe to be the core of Jesus' teaching.

Item 3 does not include reference to acts of healing except in the cases of what we might term mental illnesses. Perrin gave no support to the possibility of an instant healing of a withered hand, an enabling of a paralyzed man to stand up and walk, or other clearly miraculous acts attributed to Jesus. Instead, he mentioned that miracle stories are "known to us from every culture in the world of the New Testament" and felt that many such stories about Jesus were "originally designed as propaganda," allowing Christianity to compete with Hellenistic Greek, Syrian, Jewish, and Egyptian faiths (Perrin, 1974, p. 11). All three sources do agree, however, that Jesus was well-known as a healer of some sort.

Ehrman consistently points out that historians have no way of judging the authenticity of miracle stories—including, of course, the story of the post-crucifixion appearances. Historians deal with patterns of events, not with events that are unique, one-of-a-kind.

> [T]o agree with an ancient person, therefore, that Jesus healed the sick, walked on water, cast out demons, or raised the dead is to agree first that there were divine men (or

> magicians) walking the earth who could do such things, and second that Jesus was one of them … [F]rom a historian's perspective, anyone who believes that Jesus [performed such miracles] must be willing in principle to concede that other people did them as well, including the pagan holy man Apollonius of Tyana, the Roman emperor Vespasian, and the Jewish miracle worker Hanina ben Dosa—all of whom were reputed to be miracle workers. (Ehrman, 1999, pp. 194–95)

The Jesus Seminar scholars come at the question of miracle healings from a different perspective. A (slim) majority of the scholars believes that Jesus may have cleared up a case of "some form of dermatitis" (called "leprosy" in that culture) and that he probably cured a paralytic (Funk et al., 1998, pp. 61–64). Working as I am on the basis of God having performed some sort of miracle in the appearances of Jesus after the crucifixion, I am bolder than the Seminar scholars on this question. The way in which Jesus related to God, which in my view ultimately led to those appearances, could easily have led to not only instant cures of mental illnesses but also instant healings of a purely physical nature. These could well have been acts in which, through the agency of Jesus, God both expressed compassion for the sick and demonstrated the closeness of Jesus' relationship with God. And while Ehrman's conclusion regarding the historian's perspective is of course correct, from my perspective it does not follow at all: those other persons cannot be assumed to have had the kind of relationship with God that Jesus had.

Item 4 is supported by numerous accounts in the Synoptic Gospels of Jesus associating with the poor, the powerless, and the sick. It is possible to infer from that fact that Jesus' primary concern was *only* for the down-and-out. However, the crowds that followed him may well have included even a majority of persons of moderate class status, who were seldom mentioned in the gospels because most of what Jesus did, other than what he said, was in the nature of helping those who needed help. Surely his teachings, to which I now turn, were meant for people in general.

The Central Feature of Jesus' Teachings, in My View

The first thought in addressing the main thrust of Jesus' teachings might well be to address what he is reported to have said in the appearances. The earliest versions of the gospel of Mark contain no such appearances, so I am here addressing just the gospels of Matthew and Luke. Unfortunately, there is not much agreement between the two ascriptions. Moreover, the ascribing of a final message to Jesus is the ideal way for a gospel writer to sum up for the reader the writer's purpose of the entire gospel.

It is thus not surprising that Matthew, whose gospel consistently finds authorization for incidents in Jesus' life as the fulfillment of the Hebrew Scriptures, focuses on a new authorization in which Jesus (a) claims that all authority in heaven and on earth has now been given to him and (b) commands his disciples to baptize new followers in all nations. Nor is it a surprise that Luke has Jesus explaining the necessity of the crucifixion and saying that repentance and forgiveness of sins should be proclaimed in his name to all nations. The one common element, the need to spread Jesus' gospel to all nations, does not fit with the idea of an imminent end of the age: evangelizing all nations even in that part of the world would require a long time. This command may well have been in both "M" and "L"; possibly it goes back to something Jesus said.

Criteria Used by Biblical Scholars

What follows next is a brief examination of several criteria used by New Testament scholars in evaluating the likely authenticity of the various statements ascribed to Jesus in the gospels—that is, the likelihood that Jesus either said those things or at least might have said something like those things. I will introduce these criteria as described by Ehrman in *Jesus: Apocalyptic Prophet of the New Millennium*, since he first discusses broad criteria ("rules of thumb") and then the more widely discussed specific criteria (Ehrman, 1999, pp. 87–96, 134–137).

The first broad criterion he addresses might be called "chronological priority" and is summarized in his words as "the earlier the better." Although, as he notes, "[t]his isn't a hard and fast rule," he sees this criterion as particularly applicable to material from the ancient world, such as the world in Jesus' day (Ehrman, 1999, p. 87). The other rules of thumb are "negative": rather than proposing a feature that strengthens the argument for authenticity, they propose features that argue against it.

As a second broad criterion, Ehrman proposes that "accounts of Jesus that are clearly imbued with a highly developed theology are less likely to be historically accurate," due to the fact that "later sources tend to be more theologically oriented than earlier ones" (Ehrman, 1999, pp. 88–89).

His third rule of thumb is that doubt is cast on authenticity by a clear bias on the part of the author, as when "just about every story … drives home, either subtly or obviously, the same point" (Ehrman, 1999, p. 89).

As to more specific criteria, Ehrman cites first that of "independent attestation," meaning that more than one original source gives essentially the same account: "A strong case will be supported by several witnesses [sources] who independently agree on a point in issue" (Ehrman, 1999, p. 90). He adds words of caution, though: "This is not to deny that individual documents can provide reliable historical information." Perrin calls this the criterion of "multiple attestation," but Ehrman's title is more to the point. A saying found in all three of the Synoptic Gospels is thereby attested multiple times, but the essence of much of what is found in Matthew and Luke clearly came from Mark, which scholars say was written first.

The criterion of independent attestation is simply whether the saying occurs in some clearly recognizable form in more than one out of four or perhaps five collections of the sayings of Jesus deemed to be "primary." Each of these collections is felt by scholars to meet this standard because of evidence that it was among the very first written sources. Four sources considered to be independent have been mentioned already: the gospel of Mark, clearly a primary source for the gospels of Matthew and Luke; a presumably lost document called "Q," which was another source for both Matthew and Luke; and written material used exclusively in the writing of each of those two gospels, called, logically enough, "M" and "L." The gospel of Thomas, which was discovered in Egypt in 1945, provides no narrative context to Jesus' sayings but attests to one hundred fourteen sayings as coming from Jesus. Some scholars consider it to be a fifth independent source of things that Jesus probably said (Funk et al., 1997, p. 15). This is the source of the Jesus Seminar's book on "the five gospels."

Next Ehrman introduces what he terms "[t]he most controversial criterion that historians use, and often misuse, to establish authentic tradition from the life of Jesus [which] is sometimes called the 'criterion of dissimilarity'" (Ehrman, 1999, p. 91). "What if," Ehrman asks, "a saying or deed attributed to Jesus … does not obviously support a Christian cause, or even goes against it?" ("Christian" here refers to the theology and practice of the early Christians.) "Why … would it be preserved in the tradition? Perhaps because it really happened that way." That is, perhaps it was something—or much like something—that Jesus actually said.

Ehrman adds this comment: "The criterion of dissimilarity is best used not in the negative way of establishing what Jesus did not say or do, but in the positive way of showing what he likely did" (Ehrman, 1999, p. 92). Perrin also used this criterion, as did Funk and Hoover, who used the adjective *distinctive* instead of *dissimilar*. As an illustration of the idea, Ehrman applies this criterion to the reports of an event, as opposed to a statement by Jesus, to argue that the crucifixion must have happened. Prior to Jesus' time, "there were no Jews, at least so far as we know, who believed that the Messiah was going to be crucified," and "therefore Christians who wanted to proclaim Jesus as Messiah would not have invented the notion that he was crucified," since having to defend the concept of Messiah who had been crucified made it difficult for them to win converts from among the Jews (Ehrman, 1999, p. 93).

The application of this criterion is often controversial. Differences of opinion arise because of the possibility that a dissimilar passage might have been added by someone with an agenda that gave more weight to advancing some particular doctrine or theme than to faithfully transcribing the material provided. As noted earlier, Ehrman considers Luke 17:20–21 to be such an addition.

Another possible source of controversy regarding what is or is not dissimilar concerns Mark's account of Jesus' crucifixion. What might be considered a good candidate for authenticity is the description of the only words, according to Mark, that Jesus spoke from the cross, which is translated as part of Psalm 22—namely, "My God, my God, why have you forsaken me?" (Mark 15:34b). Many scholars, however, consider that description to be inauthentic. They feel that it was added by the early Christian movement, which was anxious to connect Jesus' sacrificial death to Hebrew Scriptures. A different or additional motivation for its inclusion may have been to comfort or reassure persecuted Christians who themselves were wondering whether God had forsaken them (Mellowes, 1998, video production, parts I and III).

The last criterion Ehrman discusses is essentially common sense. "Contextual credibility" maintains that "reliable traditions must conform to the historical and social contexts to which they relate," meaning, in the case at hand, the context of first-century Palestine (Ehrman, 1999, p. 94). This rule can be used to argue against evaluating certain sayings of Jesus to be authentic, but it provides no strong evidence favoring their authenticity. Perrin, who called this the criterion of "linguistic and environmental tests," gave an example of how it can be used. "[T]he teaching on divorce in Mark 10," he wrote, "cannot go back to Jesus in its present form because it presupposes Roman and not Jewish divorce law" (Perrin, 1974, p. 282).

Which of these six criteria should be taken as the most important ones? In *Jesus: The Apocalyptic Prophet*, Ehrman himself, while giving interesting examples of all six, seems to give a lot of weight to the first one he lists, the one I termed *chronological priority*. "Scholars of antiquity agree," he writes, "that, as a rule, we should give preference to sources that are closest to the time of the events they narrate and that are insofar as possible not tendentious" (Ehrman, 1999, p. 128). That makes a lot of sense when the narration is intended to record history for historical reasons. Those who are closest in time to whatever happened should have the most reliable memories of what actually occurred.

But as Ehrman noted, historical accuracy was not a primary motivation for the writing of the gospels. "Precisely because these documents were of such importance to people who believed in Jesus as the Son of God, their concerns, to put it somewhat simplistically, were less historical than religious. They were not interested in providing the brute facts of history for impartial observers, but in proclaiming their faith in Jesus as the Son of God" (Ehrman, 1999, p. 87).

Which criterion, then, among Ehrman's list of six, *should* be able to identify most accurately the true sayings of Jesus—those sayings that, at least in essence, represent what he actually told his followers? The criterion that seems to me to meet this challenge is that of *dissimilarity.*

Meeting the criteria of contextual credibility is, of course, a mandatory requirement for any saying to be true, but that does not point *toward* sayings; it just works *against* them. The same is true for the "negative" rules of thumb. Being free of a highly developed theology and being free of any clear bias are essential. Independent attestation is a good sign, but none of my three main sources—Ehrman, Perrin, and Jesus Seminar—seems to consider it to be essential. On the other hand, they all seem to rate the dissimilarity criterion highly. Perrin, in fact, called it "the fundamental criterion" (Perrin, 1974, p. 281).

Matthew 25:31–46

Another example Ehrman uses to illustrate this criterion will in fact introduce the crux of what I want to say in the remainder of this chapter. As he suggests, dissimilarity is especially powerful in the case of a saying attributed to Jesus that goes against early Christian theology. And that is the case with the story of the final judgment in Matthew 25. This fascinating passage deserves to be quoted in full.

> When the Son of Man comes in his glory, and all the angels with him, then he will sit on the throne of his glory. All the nations will be gathered before him, and he will separate people one from another as a shepherd separates the sheep from the goats, and he will put the sheep at his right hand and the goats at the left. Then the king will say to those at his right hand, "Come, you that are blessed by my Father, inherit the kingdom prepared for you from the foundation of the world; for I was hungry and you gave me food, I was thirsty and you gave me something to drink, I was a stranger and you welcomed me, I was naked and you gave me clothing, I was sick and you took care of me, I was in prison and you visited me."

Then the righteous will answer him, "Lord, when was it that we saw you hungry and gave you food, or thirsty and gave you something to drink? And when was it that we saw you a stranger and welcomed you, or naked and gave you clothing? And when was it that we saw you sick or in prison and visited you?" And the king will answer them, "Truly I tell you, just as you did it to one of the least of these who are members of my family, you did it to me."

Then he will say to those at his left hand, "You that are accursed, depart from me into the eternal fire prepared for the devil and his angels; for I was hungry and you gave me no food, I was thirsty and you gave me nothing to drink, I was a stranger and you did not welcome me, naked and you did not give me clothing, sick and in prison and you did not visit me."

Then they also will answer, "Lord, when was it that we saw you hungry or thirsty or a stranger or naked or sick or in prison, and did not take care of you?" Then he will answer them, "Truly I tell you, just as you did not do it to one of the

> least of these, you did not do it to me." And these will go away into eternal punishment, but the righteous into eternal life. (Matthew 25:31–46)

Ehrman devotes a full page of *Jesus: The Apocalyptic Prophet of the New Millennium* to the striking dissimilarity this story bears to the early Christian church's standard approach to salvation.

> [T]he future judgment is not based on belief in Jesus' death and resurrection, but on doing good things for those in need. Later Christians—including most notably Paul … but also the writers of the Gospels—maintained that it was belief in Jesus that would bring a person into the coming Kingdom. But nothing in this passage even hints at the need to believe in Jesus per se: these people didn't even *know* him … It doesn't seem likely that a Christian would formulate a passage in just this way. The conclusion? It probably goes back to Jesus. (Ehrman, 1999, p. 136)

I concur with this conclusion, with the proviso that I think there may well have been some editorial doctoring. As Beck proposed, "This judgment scene combines common Jewish expectations and original ideas of Jesus with expert editorial arrangement" (Beck, 1954, p. 296).

Expectations common to Judaism are reflected in the usage of the term "Son of Man," which goes back to a passage in the book of Daniel. "As I watched in the night visions, I saw one like a human being [in Aramaic, "one like a son of man"] coming with the clouds of heaven. And he came to the Ancient One and was presented before him. To him was given dominion and glory and kingship, that all peoples, nations, and languages should serve him. His dominion is an everlasting dominion that shall not pass away, and his kingship is one that shall never be destroyed" (Daniel 7:13–14).

"Son of Man" is used only at the start (v. 31). As the story proceeds, the judge is referred to as the "king," which often represents God in Matthew's versions of parables. The concept of the Son of Man as having a kingdom is found primarily in Matthew's gospel (Beck, 1954, p. 293), so editorial arrangement by Matthew may have occurred.

In this connection, the Jesus Seminar feels that the gospels' authors "frequently expand sayings or parables, or provide them with an interpretive overlay or comment" (Funk et al., 1997, p. 21), whereas what had been retained by the oral traditions tended to be "the core or gist of [Jesus'] sayings and parables" (Funk et al., 1997, p. 28). Thus it seems quite possible to me that Editor Matthew added verse 31. Nevertheless, the story's core is clearly apocalyptic overall. I will argue that it is a parable using apocalyptic imagery.

As noted earlier, the concept of the eternal consequences of a day of judgment was a "common Jewish expectation." The last chapter of Daniel prophesies that at the end of the age, "[m]any of those who sleep in the dust of the earth shall awake, some to everlasting life, and some to shame and everlasting contempt" (Daniel 12:2). Jesus' own teachings may have reflected this familiar idea as a prophecy at some stage of his ministry, or they may illustrate his use of apocalyptic imagery as a tool. But what is most important about the story, to me, is what I believe to be "original ideas of Jesus."

Neither Perrin nor the Jesus Seminar endorses Ehrman's verdict of authenticity. In a paragraph "introducing to the reader [a] particular early Christian literary form," Perrin called Matthew 25 "a chapter of eschatological parables" (Perrin, 1974, p. 79). In a later chapter, he wrote that this story "sums up many prominent themes [in Matthew's gospel]: the need for "righteousness" to enter the Kingdom; righteousness consisting of an obedience expressed in deeds; the fact that the Son of Man will repay everyone according to his deeds; the need for mercy, especially to those who are weak. It is thus a fitting climax to Matthew's presentation of the teaching of Jesus" (Perrin, 1974, p. 188).

This is noncommittal at best, in terms of any endorsement of the passage as based on what Jesus himself probably said. Funk and Hoover say outright that the story "is not a parable but a portrayal of the last judgment. The only figurative language is the simile of the sheep and the goats … The theme here is judgment and the judge is the son of Adam or the king … who will come in his glory and sit on his throne to render judgment … This all fits well into Matthew's theological scheme, which became popular in the post-Easter community. Fellows of the Seminar designated the story black [meaning 'Jesus did not say this'] by common consent" (Funk et al., 1997, p. 258).

As I have mentioned, I agree, in regard to the core of the story, with Ehrman's argument that the passage authentically represents something Jesus told. Why else would Matthew have included it? If taken seriously, it argues against the very basic claim of the early Christian church that getting right with God requires accepting Jesus as our Lord and Savior.

What qualifies as the core of the story? Briefly, viewed as a story about God, the core message is this: since God so identifies with persons in need, those who are saved are those who have cared for the needy. The Scottish scholar William Barclay beautifully described the story's image of God's closeness to the needy in these words: "If we really wish to delight a parent's heart, if we really wish to move him to gratitude indeed, then the best way to do it is to help his child. God is the great Father, and the way to delight the heart of God is to help His children, who are our fellow-men" (Barclay, 1958, p. 360).

As important as that observation is, there is, in my view, more to the story than that. First, is this story a parable or a prophecy? The answer is important if, in agreement with Perrin and the Jesus Seminar, one believes that Jesus did not prophesy about the end of the world as we know it. Although the story may have been a prophecy spoken early in Jesus' ministry, I think that at its core it is a parable. My conclusions follow Beck's middle-of-the-road approach to the "apocalyptic-prophet-or-not issue" discussed in the preface, according to which Jesus "accepted some of the apocalyptic figures of speech but was not bewitched by them. He did not proclaim his teachings by visions" (Beck, 1954, p. 289).

I believe the story to be, in its core, a parable Jesus told—not a prophecy originating in some vision he had had, but rather a vehicle to talk about what is most important *for authentic life in this world.* (I am aware that, in reaching this conclusion, I am now in disagreement with all three of my major sources as to either the origin or the nature of the story of the last judgment. To Perrin and the Jesus Seminar, it did not originate with Jesus; and to Ehrman, it was an apocalyptic prophecy made by Jesus. I think that Beck might agree with me, however.)

Claiming the story of the last judgment to be a parable instead of a prophecy eliminates from the start a couple of controversies regarding the story. One concerns the intended audience: "the nations." When considered as a prophecy, it is important to decide whether the story was directed to all Christians (assuming that "the nations" would all have been converted to Christianity), to all Gentiles (which is how the word translated here as "nations" is instead translated many times in Matthew's gospel), or to all people everywhere. However, if the story is a parable describing how to live authentically, the answer is clearly that last option.

Another point of discussion that the story naturally brings up is what persons are meant by "these who are members of my family" (or, in alternative translations, "these my brethren" or "these my brothers and sisters"). Does the phrase refer to all Jews, all Christians, all those who do God's will (as in Matthew 12:49–50), or all people with whom we could interact? If this story was a prophecy, it is important to decide who it was that his hearers needed to be sure to help! As a parable, the story surely means all those in need of help, as Barclay assumed in the quotation above.

The word *parable* comes from words that would literally translate to mean something like "alongside-thrown." It represents a story that invites hearers and readers—*all* hearers and readers—to cast the ways of dealing with life portrayed in the story alongside their own ways of dealing with life. I see the detailed description of not only the *criterion* used by the king, but also the *questions* asked by the saved and the lost as key elements in the story. The questions after all tell us about the persons being judged, and this is a portrayal that hearers or readers are invited to cast alongside their own sense of what life should be about. Other passages in the gospel of Matthew dealing directly with the last judgment—such as Matthew 8:11–12; 13:41–43, 47–

50—do not deal with specific criteria for, or reactions to, the judgments received, other than saying that the lost will weep and gnash their teeth.

I think that the story goes deeper than saying that salvation is to be found in helping those less fortunate than we are. Why are those questions given so much coverage in this story? I believe that Jesus meant them to imply something about living as God wants us to live. Consider the genuine surprise on the part of both the saved and the lost. Taken literally, the story would attribute their shock to the idea that the king had been among them, disguised as a person in great need. But taken as a *parable*, an opportunity to reexamine our own approaches to life, the story has them shocked for the more fundamental reason that they had not thought that helping those in need would be the criterion for being found acceptable. The questions they had asked represent a very realistic—a very human—reaction to that shocking development.

In some circumstances, the questions we tend to ask are simply ways of expressing our feelings of surprise in a way that is less confrontational, less challenging, than expressing them forthrightly. For example, if a college student leaves home sporting a well-trimmed haircut but returns at Christmas with shaggy hair, his mother might ask, "When did you decide to let your hair grow so long?" She is not really wanting to be told the date of his decision. She is really calling attention to the fact that he apparently had made a decision with which she is not pleased.

Similarly, it seems reasonable to conclude that, in the last judgment story, the "sheep" and the "goats" were not after the specific times at which opportunities to help others were either taken or ignored. After all, what was done was done, and what did not happen did not happen. What was really on their minds was: "Is the king (God or Christ in the parable) *really* that concerned with the down-and-out? We had no idea!" The king, in turn, responds to what is really on their minds: yes, God is really that concerned.

I think that a main point of the last judgment story is that the saved were *not* doing those acts of kindness in order to be rewarded by God or to be "saved" or to escape divine punishment. They clearly didn't know that God so identified with those persons needing help that, in some sense, God was "in" the hungry, the naked, and the imprisoned. Those who were saved did those acts because that was the way they had found to add meaning and contentment to their lives … to live life authentically. As Barclay put it, "[t]hose who helped did not think that they were helping Christ, and thus piling up eternal merit; they helped because they could not stop themselves helping. It was the natural, instinctive, quite uncalculating reaction of the loving heart" (Barclay, 1958, pp. 359–360).

Conversely, the lost, as the story goes, were also stunned. Presumably, they hadn't been doing much of anything they had considered to be wrong, and they were not aware that the "rule" was to help persons in difficult circumstances. Yet they were cursed. Why? Just for not abiding by a "rule of the game" that they did not even know? Not exactly. Had they had hearts of compassion—had they felt about the poor as they would have felt about their own family members—they would have given food to the hungry and drink to the thirsty. They would have acted that way without needing to know any rules. Again, the saved were not saved by knowing and following rules in order to be saved; they were saved by having hearts of compassion, by having developed a way of living in which compassion was to them "second nature," like the natural feeling of compassion that members of a well-functioning family have for one another.

The lost were "accursed" for the lack of doing things that, had they been more kindhearted, they would have just done naturally. (*Eternal* punishment seems to be too harsh a sentence for that offense. Had the lost been given a clear warning about the criterion to be used, they might have acted with more kindness. I consider that to be additional evidence that this story is a parable, not a prophecy. On the other hand, Matthew may have added that last verse along with the first verse. According to Funk and Hoover, "[c]onclusions are most often the place where evangelists modify" (Funk et al., 1997, p. 256).)

What seems to be implied here is definitely not a matter of helping others as a way to *earn* reconciliation with God. Acts of kindness can be done out of compassion, but they can be done instead out of a basically selfish desire to rack up merits to help gain entrance to heaven and avoid going to hell. I think God appreciates acts of mercy and kindness done for any reason, but he wants us to do them, or at least try to do them, because that is how life is most fulfilling to us. That too is a type of selfishness—at some level, whatever we decide to do is what we want to do under the circumstances at hand—but according to this parable, *that* type of selfishness is done out of motivations that are the most acceptable to God. To me, the basic message of the story is simply that God wants us to have hearts of compassion, to get our main satisfaction from helping others, and to share God's compassion, which goes out to all persons but especially to those who need help: to be, in this respect, like God.

This gets me back to the idea expressed in Chapter 6 that Jesus understood God's preference for creative justice (to whatever extent it may be reasonably applied) over attributive justice as well as over retributive justice. On this specific point of intrinsic versus extrinsic rewards, I am back in agreement with the scholars of the Jesus Seminar, who gave a "black" designation to Matthew 19:28, that verse in which Jesus tells the disciples that they will sit in judgment on the twelve tribes of Israel. Funk and Hoover comment in regard to this verse that "[t]he promise of extrinsic rewards—rewards unrelated to the thing for which they are the reward—is alien to Jesus' understanding of God's domain" (Funk et al., 1997, p. 223).

The prophecy of God's providing extrinsic rewards and punishments are at the core of apocalyptic teachings—the traditional doctrines about heaven and hell are founded on it—and it may have been an integral part of Jesus' message at some point in his ministry. But I do not believe that apocalyptic prophecy characterizes the teachings of Jesus in the later parts (at least) of his ministry.

God wants us, I believe, to do good (really, to *try* to do good) primarily for the internal reward of having tried to do good. A parent appreciates good deeds done by children who are motivated by the desire to please the parent. Even more satisfying, however, can be good deeds done out of motivations that don't directly involve the parent at all but arise from imitating the parent's behavior—from trying to be like the parent.

Supporting Passages

Independently of the strength or weakness of the case for taking the core of Matthew 25:31–46 to originate with Jesus, I see the idea of developing hearts of compassion as a major emphasis in other passages that are broadly accepted as authentically describing things Jesus taught.

According to Mark 12:28–31, Jesus held that the greatest commandments are to love God with all your heart, soul, mind, and strength and to love your neighbor as you love yourself; and I think he would probably agree that they are the commandments that caught best what full participation in the kingdom of God entails. But what we do because we are *commanded* to do it is done to keep ourselves out of trouble or to earn for ourselves some reward from the source of the command. Is that the ultimate nature of God's earthly kingdom?

The image of the kingdom given in Matthew 25:34–41, and in many other places of the gospels, is different. Persons "do the right thing" out of the desire to help their brothers and sisters and to feel the satisfaction of having helped others. To people who love others, not because they were commanded to—because that was the rule to be followed—but because they want to, it would be second nature because of the way they look at life and meaning and the way they find true contentment.

In a way, what I have claimed to be the core of that parable merges the two greatest commandments: the way to implement a love for God is to develop God's kind of compassion for our fellow humans. In writing to the Galatians and to the Romans, Paul supported this perspective. An example is Galatians 5:14, which reads, "For the whole law is summed up in a single commandment, 'You shall love your neighbor as yourself.'"

Although the Jesus Seminar disagrees, Ehrman and Perrin agree that a major theme of Jesus' preaching about the kingdom is the need to repent. Both feel that Jesus' message can (in perhaps the briefest outline) be summarized in Mark 1:15: "The time is fulfilled, and the Kingdom of God has come near [or "is at hand"]; repent, and believe in the good news."

The verb "to repent" can mean either to be sorry about something or to turn around, to turn back to a better way of life. The latter meaning seems to fit best with the theme of accepting the good news about the kingdom of God. Acceptance to participation in that kingdom entails a change of attitude about how to live.

According to Funk and Hoover, the Jesus Seminar scholars colored this verse black, feeling that "[i]n the gospels, Jesus is rarely represented as calling on people to repent" (Funk et al., 1997, p. 41). However, the need for a radical change in behavior is called for in a number of passages that the Seminar colored red or pink, indicating, respectively, that Jesus had said or had probably said something similar to the words attributed to him. Examples include Matthew 5:39 (turn the other cheek), 5:40 (give him both wraps), and the core of Matthew 5:44 (love your enemy), all of which are colored red.

So, regardless of whether Jesus had much use for the word equivalent to *repent*, all three of my chief sources imply Jesus' saying that participation in the kingdom of God involves a way of looking at life that is radically different from the customary way of his day—which is pretty much like the customary way in modern society today. I think making compassion second nature is at the core of the needed change.

Jesus may have used childlike generosity, and a child's quickness to forgive, to suggest the type of transformation needed. I continue to be amazed at the way very small children can at one moment be screaming and a minute later be peaceful and happy, with the cause for the outburst put completely behind them. The Jesus Seminar thinks that he probably said something like what is attributed to him in Mark 10:14: "Let the little children come to me; do not stop them; for it is to such as these that the kingdom of God belongs." (Ehrman implies that Jesus may well have made such a statement, but he cites Mark 10:13–16 in support of the idea that Jesus saw Kingdom people as those who "would become like little children who own nothing and can lay claim to nothing" (Ehrman, 1999, p. 169). That is of course possible.)

Consider also two well-known parables in Luke's gospel. In the story of the good Samaritan (Luke 10:30–35), the Jews who encountered the wounded traveler weighed the costs of stopping to help, and did not. By contrast, a Samaritan (one of *those* people!) "was moved with pity" and gave the man all the help he needed. In Luke 15:11–32, the father of the prodigal son had such compassion for the younger son that he would not even let the young man finish his speech of contrition—so much compassion that he angered his older son. Or consider those portions of the Sermon on the Mount that I mentioned, in which Jesus invites his followers to go far beyond what ethics would require of them: to turn the other cheek, to give both shirt and coat (Matthew 5:39–40). Are these rules for everyday life? (Israelite males in that day typically wore just two things—namely a shirt and a coat (Funk et al., 1997, p. 144).) Or are they illustrations of the breadth of compassion that Jesus wanted to his followers to try to develop?

So, in his ministry was Jesus proclaiming good news—a "gospel"? Mark claims that he was: "Now after John was arrested, Jesus came to Galilee, proclaiming the good news of God, and saying, 'The time is fulfilled, and the kingdom of God has come near; repent, and believe in the good news'" (Mark 1:14–15). Mark, however, writing in and for the early Christian movement, would specify Jesus' good news as involving the imminent end of the world as we know it. At the trial of Jesus, Mark has him saying, "I am [the Messiah]" and "you will see the Son of Man seated at the right hand of the Power" and "coming with the clouds of heaven" (Mark 14:62).

I see Jesus' message as very good news but of a different sort—news about the kingdom that God is initiating in and for this continuing world, news about what sort of kingdom it is. It is a kingdom like none other, because it runs on the power of love, not on force or the threat of penalty, or even on the promise of golden crowns.

8

How We Should Live, in My View

Compassion as Second Nature

Here I address what I think the assumptions and conclusions discussed so far in this book have most to do with life on this earth, here and now, as based on what Jesus was likely, in my opinion, to have emphasized. In other words, what is the relevance to my life—not of the conclusions about Jesus drawn by Paul and the early Christian church, but of what Jesus himself may have taught by his words and deeds?

"To make compassion for others second nature" sounds both tame and trite. But is it really? I think it is neither one.

Certainly, the call to act with compassion is commonplace for religious folk the world over. Karen Armstrong, a noted author who has studied world religions extensively, has written that in the development of "Rabbinic Judaism, Christianity, and Islam," for example, compassion became a "key element," and in fact that "all [religious traditions] have at least one strand that insists that we cannot confine our compassion to our own group: we must also reach out in some way to the stranger and the foreigner—even to the enemy" (Armstrong, 2010, pp. 31–32, 143).

However, as Armstrong implies, compassion is not so familiar a concept as to lose its power if it is taken seriously. The Charter for Compassion, whose development she spearheaded, includes the statement that "compassion impels us to work tirelessly to alleviate the suffering of our fellow creatures, to dethrone ourselves from the centre of our world … and to honour the inviolable sanctity of every single human being, treating everybody, without exception, with absolute justice, equity and respect" (Armstrong, 2010, p. 6). Taken seriously, compassion therefore calls, in many cases, for bold action. To be *second nature* for us, compassion must go broadly enough and deeply enough into our innermost ways of looking at life that helping others is one of our chief sources of joy and meaning.

Here is a place where Tillich's concept of creative justice backs up the call for true compassion. Compassion in complex modern societies involves more than charity. The way we should try to help people suffering through poor conditions of any sort is not only to provide direct assistance—food, clothing, shelter—but in addition to work creatively toward changing the societal structures that foster and maintain those poor conditions.

As mentioned earlier, in adopting the view that the story of the last judgment is a parable inviting us to compare our way of living with those who participate deeply in God's kingdom, the second-nature kind of compassion we are to develop just naturally extends to all persons everywhere. To the Israelites of the first century CE, that "everywhere" would not extend to the entire world as we know it. To us, however, it must. Where are the poorest, the most powerless, the least well clothed or housed, not only in our communities but also in our country and around the world? Can we develop compassion that goes deep into our hearts and yet that is also that wide-ranging?

Obtaining a Heart of Compassion: The First Step

From my perspective, a central part of Jesus' message has to be: "Forgive, and you will be forgiven" (Luke

6:37b). This concept is prominent in the Matthew's and Luke's versions of the Lord's Prayer and is the only concern given in that prayer that is found also in Mark's gospel (Mark 11:25). Why did Jesus put so much importance on forgiving others? Basically, it is because an unwillingness to forgive those who wrong us is an unwillingness to be in God's kingdom. The need to forgive is not so much an "entrance requirement" imposed by God as it is a condition inherent in the nature of the kingdom of God, for participation in God's kingdom *implies* a willingness to forgive. A heart unwilling to forgive is a bitter heart, and bitterness is not compatible with love. So the willingness to forgive those who wrong us is the first step in obtaining a compassionate heart, in my view.

Dostoyevsky's description of the young Alyosha in *The Brothers Karamazov* includes the ideal toward which I think we should strive. Alyosha, he wrote, "never held a grudge when someone offended him. An hour later, he would answer the offender or speak to him himself, with a trustful, friendly look, as if nothing had happened. And it wasn't that he had forgotten or, having thought it over, had decided to forgive the insult; it was simply that he no longer felt offended" (Dostoyevsky, 1970, p. 22).

There are situations in which someone is willing to forgive another but is simply unable to truly do so. For example, the parent of a child who was deliberately hurt or killed by someone may simply not be able to forgive the person in that full sense. I think that God is understanding in that situation and would continue to work with the parent, although complete success in full forgiveness could well require more than one lifetime. In such cases, participating in God's kingdom would not, in my opinion, require complete success, only continuing effort.

According to Jesus, our relationship with God should be like that of a child to a loving parent. Forgiving and serving others because we share God's compassionate love for those others is the best way to love God, just as the best way to love a human parent is to love and serve what the parent loves and serves.

A Heart of Compassion: The Implications

My feeling is that the kindnesses of a compassionate heart will extend not only to other people but also, as much as is practical, to animals beside the human variety. I feel that the manifold successes of the theory of biological evolution have an important theological implication—namely, that we should not put humanity and the rest of nature into two separate categories. We are the most advanced species (at this time), but I fail to see why we should feel, therefore, that we are the only species that counts much to God.

Two ideas from the world of science deserve mention here. First, I mentioned early in the book that a number of physical constants describing our universe have values in the definite ranges that they *must* have in order for life as we experience it to be able to evolve. The likeliest reason for this fact seems to me to be that this universe was intended to be the way it is, that it is not the result of meaningless chance.

Second, I do not claim that our understanding of either the history of the cosmos or biological evolution is perfect and complete; in all probability there will be important improvements to our understanding of those processes as years go by, for such is the way science has always progressed. But we know enough, I think, to glean an insight about how God *might* work to carry out a general plan for the development of a certain kind of universe. What science seems to me to suggest about the evolution of the universe as a whole and the evolution of species on earth is that the interplay of natural laws and chance has had a crucial role in both processes. The importance of this idea was impressed on me by

Barbour's book, *When Science Meets Religion*, in which it was frequently emphasized. Pure chance thus seems not to qualify as the likeliest explanation for either the creation of our universe or its subsequent development.

I see in this conclusion of mine significant support for my belief that all living things bear a meaningful kinship grounded in God the Creator. A sense of kinship based on the operation of pure chance seems to me to lack a strong footing, due to the absence of any meaning associated with pure chance. But my belief that God set up this universe, including its laws of nature, in such a way that living things—not necessarily us, but beings such as us—could evolve, deepens for me the sense that I am kin to all creatures. We are all creations, indirectly and in part, of the will of a parent God. All of us creatures are the members of God's extended family.

What would it mean to treat *all* creatures humanely? Do we treat the animals we use for food as we would if we kept in mind that God has compassion for them too? George Will provided an insightful essay in *Newsweek* magazine, entitled "What We Owe What We Eat," based in large part on Matthew Scully's book, *Fear Factories: The Case for Compassionate Conservatism—for Animals.* Here are some excerpts:

> The disturbing facts about industrial farming by the … livestock industry—the pain-inflicting confinements and mutilations—have economic reasons. Ameliorating them would impose production costs that consumers would pay. … Animal suffering on a vast scale should [writes Scully, a former speechwriter for President George W. Bush] be a serious issue of public policy. … [in Scully's words:] "We cannot just take from these creatures; we must give them something in return. We owe them a merciful death, and we owe them a merciful life." Says who? Well, Scully replies, those who understand "Judeo-Christian morality, whose whole logic is one of gracious condescension, or the proud learning to be humble, the higher serving the lower, and the strong protecting the weak." (Will, 2005, p. 66)

This is a reasonable starting point for a society coming to terms with the insight provided by the following words from Thomas à Kempis' *The Imitation of Christ*: "If your heart is straight with God, then every creature will appear to you as a mirror of life and a sacred scripture. No creature is so small and insignificant so as not to express and demonstrate the goodness of God."

I am personally working on that idea of valuing every creature as God's indirect—but nonetheless real—creation. If we maim or kill an animal without a really good reason, as I have done many times in the past, it may or may not cause the animal pain, depending on the type of animal. But in à Kempis' view, and now in mine, it hurts God, both for the sake of the creature and for our sake. Every time we cause needless pain or loss of life, it pulls us a little farther away from the God who, through the evolutionary process, caused that life to be, just as God caused our lives to be. (Do I still swat mosquitoes and step on roaches? I do, but there is good reason for doing so. And I try not to celebrate their deaths.)

Maybe if we practice being as kind as we reasonably can to all creatures, in the belief that they, like us, are loved by God the Father, it will even help us in the effort to develop compassion for people we will never meet—and even people whose actions we detest. Agreement with their opinions or lifestyles is, of course, not required. Whatever they say, whatever they do, they are our closest relatives in God's world, and they are loved by God just as much as we are.

Another aspect of compassion from the heart deals with future generations of our own kind and of

God's other species. This topic gets us into the current debate about the reality and the consequences of global warming. There is, among the scientific community, a clear majority who feel that global warming—or more generally, rapid and uncontrolled climate change—is real. The extent to which human activity is responsible is not fully established, but I feel that that is not a reason to drag our feet in responding to the facts that globally the climate is changing and our activity is contributing significantly to those changes. Virtually no one contests the fact that our activities are regularly dumping thousands of tons of pollutants into earth's atmosphere.

We do not know the eventual results. Is it possible that for some reason the addition of those pollutants will actually end up helping the viability of life on earth by counteracting some other change that would have even worse effects? Of course. But our responsibility is to act responsibly on the basis of our best guess as to the likeliest scenarios, to do right "as God gives us to see the right," in Lincoln's words. In the short run, the effects of climate change on the richer nations are likely to be minimal and probably positive in some areas, requiring only some relatively minor changes in our ways of living. Are we in those richer countries willing to change our lifestyles for the sake of the multitudes in poorer countries who will bear the brunt of the earliest problems?

And species that evolved as we evolved are vanishing at rates unprecedented in modern history. Is that anything to us? We can hope the answers will soon be yes, but the attitude that a college religion professor of mine described as concern for only "me and my wife and my son John and his wife, we four and no more" seems at the time of writing to be strong—in the United States, at least.

As for the long run, what about the effects three, four, and more generations from now? Many scientists think that climate change will soon reach a tipping point beyond which any current predictions of the consequences become unreliable. In that case, although the biggest effects will not occur in the lifetimes of our immediate families, they will impact generation upon generation farther down the line. Do we dare to care about those generations? If so, have we begun to act with compassion in our hearts for the inhabitants of this earth in the distant future? But, we might object, they don't even exist. Do we believe that in setting his face toward Jerusalem, Jesus acted with compassion in his heart for not only his own generation but for all generations yet to come, undetermined as they were? If so, then we should dare to care about future generations, too.

Many situations in life do, of course, impose constraints on the implementation of compassion. We may feel compassion but circumstances may make it inadvisable or even impossible to act on that feeling. At the personal level, if stopping on a lonely road to help what appears to be a person in need is clearly dangerous to oneself, the compassion felt for that person may need to be channeled into a different route, such as calling for emergency service as soon as possible.

In world affairs, the compassion one should feel for the enemy soldiers in a "just war" such as World War II cannot be allowed to prevent one from fighting for the right. The outbreak of a war rarely happens without warning, and going to war should be averted at almost any cost. If, in spite of all reasonable efforts to prevent it, a war starts, possibilities for compassionate action toward the enemy forces are severely limited. Such circumstances should, however, not get us out of a habit of such action when circumstances do permit it. After all, another way to look at those hardnosed decisions is this: compassion should ultimately lead us to work to promote the greater good for the greater number. Losing one's life to a robber on a lonely road or to an enemy soldier in a just war effort does not meet that criterion.

And even in wartime, compassion at times can be shown—and often *is* shown—to enemy troops who, like us, are children of God.

Taken seriously, making compassion for others *truly* our second nature is neither tame nor trite. In fact, the question is: is it possible? Probably not completely, and certainly not all the time. But we can make it a habit to strive toward that level of compassion. And of course we can ask for help from the Holy Spirit.

As I suggested above in terms of dealing with animals, I think a deep sense of kinship is helpful. The same applies even more strongly, of course, in regard to our fellow human beings. In the parable of the last judgment, the king so identified with the "least of these members of my family" that he felt personally whatever kindness was extended to them. And the "saved" had not acted out of a sense of obligation to do the right thing. If that had been their primary motivation, they would not have been surprised that being kindhearted was so important to the king. The compassion they felt as they ministered to those less fortunate than themselves might well have come from identifying with those needy persons as fellow human beings.

In the parable of the good Samaritan, Jesus contrasted a lack of identification with the injured traveler on the part of religious folk with a presumably immediate sense of pity for the plight of a fellow traveler on the Samaritan's part.

Compassion in the long term can, of course, suffer from burnout. Surely a sense of gratitude can help to sustain our compassion for others. I am fully aware that I am far, far more blessed than most of the world's population in respect to health and wealth, but we all have much to be thankful for, and reflecting on how fortunate we are can prompt us to practice compassion. One need not even believe in God to be appreciative of the blessings of life. Indeed, I know some very compassionate persons who do not believe in God but who do appreciate how good life has been to them and who, out of compassion, seek the good for other people and other living things. In my opinion, they do God's will, and almost assuredly better than I do.

Henry Ruark, who decades ago was a much-beloved Methodist minister of the church of which I am now a member, once wrote a meditation on the last judgment. He quoted a description of "a shoemaker who was skeptical as to creeds but full of helpfulness to his neighbors." He "spent his breath in proving that

God did not exist, but spent his life in proving that he did." In response, Ruark commented that "[i]n the choice between [two approaches to religion] there is no question which kind of religion the Master would approve"—the shoemaker's or the religion of one whose stated beliefs do not "issue in a certain quality of life."

"What Jesus was concerned with was not 'technical' Christians. Certainly he considered belief important, for our beliefs finally determine how we live. But no belief is real that does not issue in a certain quality of life … He gave to religion a central place, for a man's inheritance in the kingdom depends at last on his relationship to Jesus: 'you did it unto me.' But the genuineness of that relationship is evidenced in a man's kindliness to 'the least of these my brethren'" (Ruark, 1960, p. 35).

This quotation supports my belief that the gospel of Jesus has relevance that reaches beyond traditional forms of Christianity, relevance that applies in fact to the entire world. Those who believe in God understand humanity's common kinship in terms of their belief in and thankfulness for the meaningful work of a beneficent God. The idea that we learn to give love to others because God has first loved us is not confined to any one theistic religion. This might, in general, tend to give theists a more resilient commitment to compassionate intentions and actions as compared to agnostics and atheists who, I suppose, think of humanity's kinship as the result of pure chance. For example, some people claim that everyone on earth has the right to a decent life. A cynic might ask, "Says who?" Those of us who believe that the ultimate source of all our lives is a God who loves us all equally have, I believe, a stronger answer than non-theists have and might therefore be more inclined to fight for the implementation of that right.

However, I do believe that God values compassionate intentions and actions, regardless of one's religious affiliation, if any. Those intentions and actions are godlike, after all.

9

A Synopsis and Concluding Thoughts

Some people believe that science progresses by way of experiments and observations leading to hypotheses that are first proposed and subsequently proved or disproved. In actuality the process is much more complex—bordering at times on chaotic—and in the end hypotheses are never proved, in the sense of being placed on a pedestal with no further testing needed. Scientists seek theories providing *the likeliest explanations* of the results obtained under the types of circumstances that have been examined. If confirmation is achieved of new results that do not agree with those likeliest explanations, any of several things may happen: the original theory may be modified; it may eventually be considered as providing fairly accurate approximations only in the original realm for which it was designed; or it may be abandoned.

But in any case, a new theory emerges that provides the likeliest explanations of both the original results and the new results.

When I try to follow the same procedure in deciding what I should believe about the big questions of life, I end up believing in the kind of God that Jesus is said to have described in his non-apocalyptic teachings—and in that God's divine intervention—as the likeliest explanation of the alleged appearances of Jesus after his crucifixion. As I noted at the outset, I have other reasons as well for belief in Jesus' picture of God as I understand it to have been, but to me the clearest image is in what I believe Jesus taught, coupled with the confirmation of that message by the post-crucifixion appearances.

As I discussed early in Chapter 1, part of the reasoning behind my beliefs is based on science. I consider the likeliest explanation for our universe supporting life as we know it to be that this specific kind of universe was willed. I am aware that some people would conclude from that belief that there may be a God, but if so, God is not worthy of worship. In Appendix 2, I will address my ideas about various ways in which a God both powerful and good might respond to all the pain and evil in this world.

Also in Chapter 1, I discussed my conviction that God could directly intervene in natural processes and human affairs, because laws of nature do not command what must happen but rather describe what normally happens. If, as I believe, there is a Creator of the universe, that Creator is not limited by the laws of nature describing that universe. That just seems logical to me.

Chapter 2 gives my reasons for focusing, in some later chapters, on primarily the non-apocalyptic teachings ascribed to Jesus in the Synoptic Gospels. A conclusion I draw in Chapter 5 reinforces that decision, in the sense that I do not think that Jesus so misunderstood God's will that, at least in the latter part of his ministry, he was incorrectly predicting an imminent end of the world as we know it. In Chapter 2, I also discuss the possibility that Jesus' message changed at some point in his ministry. In my opinion, it very likely did, from apocalyptic to non-apocalyptic.

Chapter 3 focuses on four statements, all generally recognized as historically accurate. Given those facts, my belief in a God both powerful and good, and the possibility of divine interventions in our world, the likeliest explanation of the claimed post-crucifixion appearances of Jesus is, for me, that they were in fact the result of divine intervention. As described in Chapter 4, I cannot see any likelier explanation of why some of those who had followed Jesus prior to his crucifixion—plus his brother James and especially Paul—apparently spread the good news of what they believed to be Jesus' resurrection in spite of potentially lethal opposition.

Chapter 5 begins the discussion of my personal beliefs concerning the likeliest explanation of why God intervened in that way. These beliefs are heavily dependent on a lifetime of experiences, a lifetime that has been extremely easy compared to the lives of most of the rest of the world. The rest of the book also represents my personal views alone.

I believe that God wanted both to honor Jesus' life and his willingness to die for the sake of God's kingdom on earth, and to allow Jesus' own gospel to spread to Jews and Gentiles alike. I believe that, in order for the gospel message to get a foothold beyond Israel, God sent Paul and others out into the Gentile world with a message that belief in Jesus would lead to eternal blessings rather than unending condemnation in the next life.

In Chapter 6, I discuss my views on how Jesus' gospel and Paul's gospel relate to each other. I am doubtful that *eternal* condemnation is a possibility; in any case, if God does provide attributive and retributive justice in the next life, I believe that acceptance of Paul's gospel of salvation by faith suffices to ensure that the justice received is not eternal punishment. Jesus' *own* gospel, in my view, focuses on how to live as God wants us to live in this world; and I do not think that Paul's gospel of salvation replaces Jesus' gospel of the reconciliation that God offers us. In my view, reconciliation implies salvation; and reconciliation, according to Jesus, is obtained by forgiving our debtors, asking God to forgive us of our own sins, and honestly trying not to repeat them.

Chapter 7 concerns my view of the focus of Jesus' teaching, both by word and by deed, about how to live in the here and now. I think that the emphasis was on developing heartfelt compassion, translated into helping the needy wherever and whenever it is possible. As I see it, compassion as second nature and the actions to which it leads fulfill—with *fulfill* meaning "to achieve the purpose of"—the commandment to love your neighbor, meaning everyone. At the same time, it fulfills the commandment to love God, for there is no way to better please a perfect parent than to adopt toward the parent's other children the same compassionate attitude that the parent has. Surely no teaching could be more relevant than this one to the challenges we face in today's world, as I discussed in Chapter 8.

I do not claim to have presented any truly new perspectives in these chapters. In the centuries since Jesus' time on earth, everything that I have explored in these pages has probably been explored—and explored better, in fact—by others. I may have put the pieces together in a slightly different way. In any case, early in the preface I stated that "my goal in the book is to present as strong a case as I can in support of two beliefs that I hold: (1) that God, pictured much as Jesus described God in his teachings, was directly responsible for some post-crucifixion appearances of Jesus; and (2) that in so acting, God validated that part of Jesus' own gospel—the message he gave through both his words and his deeds—which is most relevant to today's world." That is what I have attempted to do.

A few words are in order here, regarding the so-called "social gospel" that developed in the first part of the twentieth century. In *The Scandalous Gospel of Jesus*, Gomes noted that the social gospel arose at a time in which orthodoxy and modernity were competing with each other to be the dominant religious movement in America. The social gospel offered, Gomes said, a third way in which proponents of both sides should be able to agree. "Who could argue with the mandate 'Thy kingdom come, thy will be done on *earth* as it is in heaven'? Presumably, [both sides] could agree that Jesus' social mandate for the 'least of these' was meant to be tried out here on earth." Gomes quoted Walter Rauschenbusch, widely held to be the social gospel's "father," as stating that "It is not a matter of getting individuals into heaven, but of transforming the life on earth into the kingdom of heaven." As the twentieth century wore on, the social gospel movement lost strength, but Gomes asked the reader, "Has its time come again?" (Gomes, 2007, pp. 174–175).

A major problem faced by that movement was the initial optimism with which it was infused. World War I, which ended the year after Rauschenbusch's death, proved not to be the war that would end all wars: far from it. According to Gomes, as the twentieth century wore on, the social gospel "could not survive the stresses of the religious life in a cynical, selfish, and partisan age" (Gomes, 2007, p. 175). The current age has those same characteristics to a large degree, but I think that the time has come for a more realistic, humbler social gospel. Life on earth will not fully become the kingdom of heaven as long as people are human, but at least we can hope for a world far better world than it is. In my view, Jesus' own gospel is a social gospel.

APPENDIX 1:

The Role of the Crucifixion, from My Perspective

The direct cause of Jesus' crucifixion was the carrying out of orders prompted by the opposition to Jesus of the temple authorities in conjunction with the Roman authorities' desire to keep any uprisings from developing. Certainly God could have prevented the crucifixion in the first place; so why did that not happen? Why did God let such a good man die so cruel a death? I believe God allowed Jesus to go to the cross in order to save us from our sins.

Jesus himself may or may not have felt that his crucifixion would satisfy God's need for blood sacrifice to pay for humanity's sinfulness. He may instead have chosen to let himself be sacrificed in order to free those who would believe his teachings from the bondage of sin and guilt. His main purpose may not have been to pay a debt to a God requiring that someone be punished for the world's sins, but rather to be "a ransom for many" (Mark 10:45) in the usual sense of a ransom paid—often to an unsavory character such as a kidnapper—to free a captive. In this case, the captor is our innate sense that seriously sinful behavior cannot go unpunished. If there is a Satan external to our minds, he certainly pushes that idea. Some people, following a familiar Christmas carol, might in fact consider Jesus' death a ransom paid "to free us all from Satan's power," not from the wrath of a vengeful God.

In *Mark as Story: An Introduction to the Narrative of a Gospel*, professors David Rhoads, Joanna Dewey, and Donald Michie describe their understanding of what the writer of the earliest of the gospels thought about the meaning of the crucifixion.

> Mark does not portray Jesus' death as a sacrifice for sin. Mark portrays Jesus already pardoning sin during his life and empowering others in the same way. His death is not needed to make forgiveness possible.…
>
> Twice the Markan Jesus suggests an interpretation [of Jesus' death]. First, Jesus

> suggests it is an act of service that is a "ransom for many." The word "ransom" was not part of the language of sacrifice but a term that depicted the release of a slave or a hostage. That is, in Mark, Jesus sees his whole life, including his execution, as a means by which people are ransomed or liberated for a life of service in the rule of God. …
>
> Second, at the final Passover meal, Jesus portrays his execution as sealing a covenant. … Covenants in antiquity were ratified by pouring blood from a sacrifice on both parties to the covenant. Thus the narrator presents Jesus asking, if you will, that his execution seal the covenant of the rule of God with "the many," the new community of Judeans and Gentiles alike who follow Jesus in the way of service and who are also willing, if need be, to stand in opposition to the government and risk the consequences. (Rhoads, Dewey, and Michie, 1999, pp. 113–114)

I discussed earlier my view that Jesus taught that God is willing to forgive sinful behavior—behavior causing deliberate estrangement from God or from our fellow humans—without some sort of punishment. According to Jesus, a right relationship with God—participation in God's kingdom—begins simply with an attitude of forgiveness toward others and the request to be forgiven oneself, coupled with determination to do better in the future. This was in direct opposition to the teachings of the Pharisees, who held that a right relationship with God was possible only by observing all the laws attributed to Moses, and that those persons who would not or could not keep those laws were beyond hope of reconciliation. Jesus saw full participation in the kingdom of God as providing the fulfillment of the Mosaic laws, in the sense that it meets the goal of those laws.

We today do not have Pharisees with whom to contend. However, many of those laws of Moses demanded severe punishments, including death sentences, for offenders in this life. In our own day, we generally apply that same retributive sense of justice to the needs of society, where punishment is often held to be necessary as a corrective, and sometimes—wrongly, I believe—as vengeance. It is therefore understandable that we should tend to attribute to God the demand for retributive justice in this world or the next for human sinfulness, even though in the standard Christian tradition those persons who are sent to a fiery hell suffer unending punishment as God's vengeance. (A negative effect of this tradition is that some Christians seem to think of their faith as primarily "fire insurance.") Jesus himself probably described God in this way at times (as in the parable of the last judgment) to emphasize that certain types of conduct are not tolerated in God's kingdom. Of course, he may also have accepted as literally true the concept that God demands retributive justice.

In any case, our holding that concept to be true can easily thwart God's will for us. We are so accustomed to the practice of retributive justice in human affairs that we tend to feel (subconsciously, at least) that forgiveness without penalty is not good enough—not even good enough for us to forgive ourselves. Our sense of pride strengthens this feeling: we know we *should* have done better, but we *failed*. Thus we see ourselves as unclean, and the result is further self-imposed alienation from God. This sense of unworthiness, this burden of past sins, is especially likely in those who try to live up to what Jesus taught about how we should approach life. We often fail miserably in our attempts to acquire the attitudes set forth in the Sermon on the Mount and other such teachings. This, incidentally, is a major reason for the importance of the church, the synagogue or temple, and the mosque, in which we sinners come together to worship God but also to acknowledge our sinfulness, to celebrate God's forgiveness, and to be reenergized in our efforts to live as we ought to live.

In *God and the World*, Cobb sees an innate reluctance to make a change in one's behavior due to the weight (I would call it the momentum) that past occasions, as they have turned out, carry into each new moment. This momentum affects our decisions profoundly, and although it does not, of course, determine them completely, it often leads to poor decisions:

"God is the One Who Calls us beyond all that we have become to what we might be. Clearly, we are not to understand every event as simply the embodiment of the ideal that is offered to it. The power of our own past over us in each new present is immense … It is easier to ignore the lure of God than to overcome the weight of that past; hence the appalling slowness of our progress toward full humanity and the ever-impending possibility that we turn away from it catastrophically" (Cobb, 1969, p. 82).

Moreover, our focus on retributive justice makes it difficult for us to accept God's forgiveness of others—especially those whose sinfulness exceeds, in our opinion, our own. This too has become human nature, and it works against any desire to forgive our debtors.

C. S. Lewis' *The Great Divorce* is full of parables that invite readers to reexamine the ways in which they look at things. In one, a resident of hell, who is presently a guest in heaven and is free to remain there, rejects the opportunity to stay because he doesn't want to be in the same place as a murderer. "If they choose to let in a bloody murderer all because he makes a poor mouth at the last moment, that's their lookout. But I don't see myself going in the same boat with you, see? Why should I? I don't want charity. I'm a decent man and if I had my rights I'd have been here long ago and you can tell them I said so" (Lewis, 1946, p. 34).

But the Hebrew psalmist proclaimed that "[God] does not deal with us according to our sins, nor repay us according to our iniquities. For as the heavens are high above the earth, so great is his steadfast love to those who fear him [i.e., worship him and try to obey him]; as far as the east is from the west, so far he removes our transgressions from us" (Psalm 103:11–12). That, in my opinion, is as true today as it was when it was composed, and it applies to everyone. A new feature in Jesus' own message is added insight in regard to what trying to obey God's will entails. Jesus proclaimed an emphasis on asking to be forgiven *when we have forgiven our debtors.* Although willingness to forgive others is not a major emphasis in the Hebrew Bible, it is certainly implied in the Golden Rule, which is incorporated in some form in all the major world religions (Armstrong, 2010, p. 4).

So, I think that it *may* have been largely in response to the difficulty we tend to have in *accepting* God's freely given forgiveness, both for ourselves and for others, that Jesus decided to let himself be executed and that God decided to allow the crucifixion to occur.

One way of interpreting the parable of the dishonest manager (Luke 16:1–8) supports this possibility. In that parable, a rich master tells his manager that he is being fired. The manager then figures out how he will get along without his job: before leaving it, he will call in people who owe debts to his master and will allow them to reduce their bills—so that they will in turn help him out later on. The end of the parable is a shocker: the rich master commends his manager for being so shrewd! Since a parable is a story that the hearers should reflect on in comparison with their own lifestyles, the implicit question is what we might make out of this curious ending. One answer is that we may need to rethink what pleases God. The parable suggests that secular people can be more alert to the kinds of activity that please their masters than religious people are inclined to be. Rather than disbelieving in the opportunity for reconciliation with God because of how poorly they themselves or others have acted, people can please God regardless of their past by forgiving themselves and others, asking for God's forgiveness, and moving on with determination to do better.

Ehrman points out—correctly, in my view—that Jesus was "particularly concerned in bringing in those who are lost and in need into the Kingdom" (Ehrman, 1999, p. 151.) One passage he cites in support is Mark 2:17, and the Jesus Seminar scholars agree that Jesus may well have repeated this secular saying that it is the sick who need a doctor. If he did, perhaps Jesus had in mind not only those who, in his culture, were outcast as lepers but also those persons of any place and time who feel unworthy even to seek reconciliation with God. A beloved African-American spiritual assures us that there is a cure for "the sin-sick soul." The Pharisees, of course, had the opposite problem: they held far too high an opinion of their own righteousness, as the parable of the Pharisee and the tax collector indicates (Luke 18:9–14). That, I feel, is part of the reason behind their antagonism to the message Jesus was providing.

If, on the other hand, Jesus did feel that retributive justice was necessary to satisfy God for humanity's reconciliation, he probably saw himself as a personification of Isaiah's vision of a suffering servant. In "Second Isaiah" (Isaiah 40–55:13), the speaker pictures the exiled Judeans as having suffered *double* the amount that would be required as a just retribution for their communal sins (Isaiah 40:2). This Isaiah claimed that God planned to bring the people back from exile and reestablish Judah as a wonderful kingdom, "a light to the nations" (Isaiah 49:6), and that by so doing, God would show the other nations the way to a better life.

But in order for the other nations' sins to be forgiven, in Isaiah's view, Israel had first been punished on their behalf. Isaiah has the nations responding as follows: "Surely [Israel] has borne our infirmities and carried our diseases; yet we accounted him stricken, struck down by God, and afflicted. But he was wounded for our transgressions, crushed for our iniquities; upon him was the punishment that made us whole, and by his bruises we are healed" (Isaiah 53:4–5).

From the outset, early Christianity developed an understanding of Jesus' suffering and death as having paid our debt to God, thereby fulfilling a need for retributive justice to be carried out. Nevertheless, I should note that although Paul often described the crucifixion as paying our debts to God, he wrote also of God's acting through Jesus to free us from bondage to sin. To the Romans, he wrote, "But thanks be to God that you, having once been slaves of sin, have become obedient from the heart to the form of teaching ["probably the gospel tradition" (Meeks, 1993, p. 2124)] to which you were entrusted, and that you, having been set free from sin, have become slaves of righteousness" (Romans 6:17–18). (McLaren notes that Paul "throws down metaphor after metaphor" as he addresses his theme (McLaren, 2010, p. 145).)

For Jesus to have decided to allow himself to be crucified would not necessarily mean that he himself saw his impending suffering and death as necessary to satisfy a need God had for retributive justice. Indeed, to see God in that way would go against much of what I believe to be what Jesus emphasized in his teaching—at least, what I think he emphasized in the later stages of his ministry. Not only does it give retributive justice priority over creative, transforming justice, but also it presents an image of God as either vengeful or as powerless to break rules laid down by God's self. That is not the way Jesus seems, to me, to have understood the nature of God's relationship to humanity.

But in any case, he must have realized how hard it would be for most people to accept the simple message of God's eagerness to welcome sinners into a familial relationship if they would forgive their debtors and, intending to do better in the future, seek forgiveness of their own sins.

This approach is both similar and dissimilar to the famous understanding of the significance of Jesus' crucifixion proposed by the eleventh-century scholar Abélard. According to William Hordern's *A Layman's Guide to Protestant Theology*, Abélard described the crucifixion as a solution to the problem that a fellowship cannot be restored—that is, reconciliation is not possible—unless the person needing forgiveness wants to be forgiven. I agree with Abélard's belief that "there was nothing on God's side that made forgiveness impossible." Hordern continues: "But forgiveness is a two-way affair … Forgiveness means the restoration of broken fellowship; but one cannot restore the fellowship if the other does not wish it restored." In response, Abélard claimed that God "sent his Son to suffer and die … as a manifestation of God's great love. When a man sees this he is moved to shame and repents," thereby making God "able to forgive him" (Hordern, 1968, p. 27).

The "orthodox argument" opposing this idea is that the crucifixion "can only be a revelation of God's love for man if it was a necessary sacrifice" rather than merely "a grand gesture" (Hordern, 1968, p. 28).

For my part, while I agree with Abélard that for salvation—in the sense of being reconciled with God—Jesus' sacrificial death is not necessary because of God's nature, I consider it to be virtually necessary because our nature. I differ with Abélard in that I base the significance of Jesus' crucifixion not on our being moved to shame but rather on our need to discard our innate focus on retributive justice. That is, the problem as I see it isn't our lack of interest in being saved but our tendency to believe that a full pardon for sin is impossible without either blood sacrifice or some sort of personal punishment.

Nevertheless, Abélard made an important point regarding our reaction to the crucifixion. Seeing, in our mind's eye, the suffering of Jesus on the cross reminds us that God's grace is not cheap. For, regardless of what Jesus understood his impending crucifixion to accomplish, he felt it necessary to face death on the cross in order to help others participate in the kingdom of God, and God felt it necessary to let him be crucified.

The realization of those facts calls for a response in how we live our lives.

In my opinion, the crucifixion of Jesus shows that God wants reconciliation with humanity—whether or not we believe that, in God's dealing with humanity, creative justice trumps retributive justice—and that *out of love for humanity, God was willing to let Jesus make any need for retributive justice a non-issue.*

It was compassion that carried Jesus to Jerusalem. I do not know whether his purpose was to pay in our place a debt that we all owe before we can be accepted into God's kingdom, or whether it was simply to convince us all that God wants us all to live in the kingdom in spite of the sins of our past. But either way, he was acting out of compassion for the people of his generation and, I believe, all generations to come.

APPENDIX 2:

How I Understand the Reasons for Suffering and Death

There are people for whom this book's whole approach is undermined by an inability to believe in a good and powerful God because of all the pain and evil in the world, both now and since time immemorial. This appendix mentions some practical reasons for the fact of suffering and death in this world and goes on to suggest why God doesn't prevent even the most egregious cases of their occurrence. In regard to the latter topic, I explore some imagery created by Cobb and by Tillich that builds on the idea that, in the life hereafter, God may extend creative justice to us, rather than the attributive justice of heaven or the retributive justice of hell.

Many people believe that all events, even great tragedies, are part of God's plan. As I indicated in Chapter 1, I follow Cobb's belief that God's acts are usually persuasive, not coercive. I believe that God has a best choice for each decision we make, but that the decisions are up to us; the future is truly open. In my view, God's plans are thus normally modified as appropriate in accordance with what we decide; whatever happens in the natural world also normally modifies God's plans.

In Chapter 8, I noted my support of Barbour's emphasis that our universe is largely a product of the combination of the workings of natural law and chance. In discussing quantum theory in Chapter 1, I emphasized the idea that true laws of nature may in fact *incorporate* chance. The wave function describing an electron may be a fundamental description of the likelihood of locating the electron at a position within a certain region of space during a certain time interval. That wave function develops in accordance with a law, but there may be no law that determines precisely where the electron lands.

Although I have argued in previous chapters for the direct intervention of God in the appearances of Jesus, I feel that the manifold successes of science indicate clearly that God has shown and continues to show great restraint in interfering with the operations of the laws of nature, including perhaps laws of chance. As seen from the vast majority of events in our times, our understanding of those laws describes what happens very well indeed. And at the level of our daily lives, that which follows any initial condition is a mixture including the termination of both good and bad possibilities and the creation of other possibilities, both good and bad. God generally lets events both good and bad—even wars and tsunamis—happen, and the world moves on, normally uninterrupted by divine intervention. The big question is, Why?

Some Partial Answers

One way that I find helpful in understanding the presence of all the pain and suffering in the world comes from the image of God in the parable of the last judgment. God so identifies with us that in some sense God must be inside us, sharing our deepest feelings, including our deepest hurts. God is thus pictured as the one who identifies with the suffering of all, sharing their pain, much as a parent suffers with the misfortunes of her children. This, of course, is not a new idea, but it has become more prominent in recent decades.

To quote Arthur Peacocke, the late biochemist and theologian: “There has, in fact, been increasing assent in the Christian theology of recent decades to the idea that it is possible to speak consistently of a God who suffers above all others and yet is still God” (Peacocke, 2001, p. 86). This image does not resolve the issue of suffering, however. The question remains as to why a good God would allow so much suffering and so many lost opportunities for good that plague our world in the first place. To claim that God suffers even more than we do is only part of a good answer.

Pain, Death, and Evolution

In 1850 Alfred, Lord Tennyson used the phrase “Nature, red in tooth and claw” to portray a truth: in the natural world, including humanity, pain and death can be found virtually everywhere, all the time. What kind of a God would devise a world in which all higher forms of life depend on the death of other life, and the process of dying is often filled with needless pain?

The earliest form or forms of life on earth could not have relied on other life for their existence, but evolution soon began giving the advantage to many life forms that did prey on other, mostly lower, forms. I think God sought the rise of intelligent life forms, types that could care for one another and protect one another and ultimately develop a sense of the holy. Maybe there are planets in the universe where all life forms coexist without one type feeding on another type. On this planet, however, God has allowed herbivores, carnivores, and omnivores to develop, hoping to see, in this context, expressions of caring and love that otherwise might have no chance to develop.

As for the prevalence of pain in the natural world, my thoughts run along similar lines. Evolution favored those individual animals that were sensitive to negative feedback from such things as eating bad food and touching a red-hot coal. And maybe on some planets, pain as we know it does not exist. But here, God has let pain develop as a warning that something bad is happening. God does not want individuals to hurt but does accept the potential for hurting to be present in order to set the stage for caring and love in ways that may not be possible in a pain-free world. Theologian John Cobb, Jr. has pointed out that evolution has wrought rapid changes that "on the whole were in the direction of richer varieties of life, more possibilities of intensity of feeling, consciousness, and freedom, in short, of greater realizations of value." (Cobb, 1969, p. 92)

More Thoughts on Disastrous Events, Large and Small

Disasters also cause pain and death. Even if pain and death are accepted as necessary in day-to-day life as we know it to be, there seem to be no adequate reasons for catastrophes, whether man-made or from natural sources. Should not a good and loving God prevent wars, disastrous earthquakes, and such?

Part of an answer can surely be found in Barbour's book, *Religion in an Age of Science*. "[Human] freedom requires a genuine choice of good or evil, and therefore [to provide free will] God had to allow the possibility that individuals would choose evil. In a world of mutual interdependence, those choices could hurt other individuals (even on the scale of the Holocaust)" (Barbour, 1990, p. 239).

And in regard to natural disasters, Barbour emphasized the need for natural laws to be maintained. "There must be dependable regularities in the world if we are to make responsible decisions about the consequences of our actions. ... Moreover, the growth of human knowledge would be impossible without the existence of such regularities. Neither moral character nor scientific knowledge would be possible if God intervened frequently to save us from suffering. Earthquake disasters and cancer are products of such natural laws, not the result of divine punishment" (Barbour, 1990, pp. 239–240).

True enough, but still, why would God not make exceptions to prevent the worst events?

I have argued for one set of direct interventions—the appearances of Jesus shortly after the crucifixion—but I do see reasons against direct, large-scale interventions in this modern age.

If there were such interventions, events such as the Holocaust and the catastrophic tsunamis of 2004 and 2011 would never have happened. In that case, though, how could God choose when *not* to intervene, if—as I believe—God has unlimited compassion for every human being? Moreover, God would become directly responsible for all the tragedies that *did* occur, by having chosen not to prevent them but preventing others.

But then, why would God allow any catastrophes at all? Clearly a beneficent and powerful God could have avoided the necessity of choosing when to intervene by intervening to prevent *all* significant errors, *all* significant pain, and *all* death. Traditionally, Christians have envisioned, for the next life of those who attain it, a world similar to that—a heaven such as is described in the book of Revelation: "[God] will wipe every tear from their eyes. Death will be no more; mourning and crying and pain will be no more, for the first things have passed away" (Revelation 21:4). A God both powerful and good could surely have set up the present world that way!

Methodist minister James C. Howell once wrote that God hopes for love and tolerates the pain and death of individuals for the sake of love. "God could have created a perfect world, peopled with perfect beings, with no illness, no evil, no flaws, no death. But God is more interested in love than in perfection. … God runs the risk of pain and suffering, hoping for love" (Howell, 1994, p. 13A).

Moreover, the idea of an error-free world runs into trouble in regard to how life in such a world is perceived by the people in it. There would be trouble, regardless of whether those constant interventions were or were not recognizable as the work of a supernatural agent.

In a world in which God's constant interventions *were* hidden, there would be for the inhabitants no character development; no need for courage or compassion, since no one gets seriously hurt; no need to forgive or to become better persons because of terrible mistakes; no chance for love to be strengthened by enduring hard times, since every endeavor would "just happen" to turn out just fine for everyone involved.

If, on the other hand, God chose to be known by constant interventions, all the modern world would behave in such a way as to please this powerful, beneficent God in order to escape punishment and to be rewarded. Religion would not be a matter of seeking to do God's will out of love for God, nor would it be a matter of trying to help others out of love for one's neighbor. Good behavior would be the only logical way to act, and religion would become a business, with God as the boss. The old idea, prominent in some books of the Hebrew Bible, that good people will prosper and bad people will suffer, would be true all the time, all over the world. That is obviously not the type of world that God wants.

As for the occurrence of natural disasters, Howell noted that in our admiration of earth's natural beauty, we tend to forget that "tornados and earthquakes are part of the package" (Howell, 1994, p. 13A).

In my opinion, the thoughts expressed by Barbour and Howell are important responses to the ages-old problem of why evil and suffering are part of our world.

Cobb's Views

In a chapter entitled "Evil and the Power of God" in Cobb's *God and the World*, the author argues that the use of "power to compel or to force" in interpersonal relationships is a "last resort which expresses ... total powerlessness in all ways that matter" (Cobb, 1969, p. 89).

Power that matters is the power of persuasion, and "God in every moment works with and upon the world that is given to him in that moment," both by willing that moment into being and by exerting upon it a formative (but not determinative) power of persuasion. "We must think of God's new act of persuasion in each moment as conditioned by just that world that he there confronts. That world, in turn, of course, reflects the influence of God's earlier persuasion, but it is not identical with what he willed it to be. And the world that God will confront in the next moment, although influenced by his present persuasion, will not fully embody even the very relative ideal he offers it now" (Cobb, 1969, pp. 91–92).

Cobb sees cosmological and biological evolution in this light, arguing that "[i]n this context the problem of natural evil in the usual sense is not acute. The destruction of living things by earthquakes and volcanoes could have been avoided only by vast postponement of the creation of life until a much higher degree of physical order was attained. But in spite of occasional destructive outbreaks there is far more value in a world teeming with life than in a dead one. And perhaps if life had waited for a safer environment, the only moment when the emergence of life on our planet was possible would have long since been past" (Cobb, 1969, p. 93).

Human error and human evil had been discussed in Cobb's preceding chapter, but along very similar lines. As I discussed in Appendix 1, Cobb sees a major problem in our tendency to be consistent with our past rather than to accept God's guidance to a better future: "It is easier to ignore the lure of God than to overcome the weight of that past; hence the appalling slowness of our progress toward full humanity and the ever-impending possibility that we turn away from it catastrophically" (Cobb, 1969, p. 82).

Ultimately, Cobb's chapter on evil winds up discussing grounds for hope, claiming that "faith in God and hope for [a better] future" are "deeply interdependent," and "[t]he minimum hope that sustains and is sustained by belief in God is that the past is not lost, that achieved value is cumulative" (Cobb, 1969, p. 98).

However, Cobb discusses two concerns. The achieved value being simply remembered—even if remembered by God—seems to lack the ability to engender much hope. "Belief that all values are preserved cumulatively in God adds importance to the realization of value, but it mocks me nevertheless at the point at which I care the most. More important than the value achieved is the person himself as a subject of new experience. It is of some importance that the old experiences are remembered, but the pathos is not thereby removed. The pathos is peculiarly acute when we think of a man who gives his life for others, asking no reward for himself" (Cobb, 1969, p. 100).

In his next paragraph, he brings up another concern. "Much [difficulty or uneasiness] holds also of hope for a better future lying ahead for mankind or for whatever succeeds mankind in the evolutionary development. Such a possibility does [give the present struggle] meaning which partly redeems suffering from horror. … [But what about] all the hundreds of millions who are condemned to perish in the desert before humanity enters the promised land? We who live in comfort and security … may pride ourselves on not demanding anything more of God. But can we equally accept the fate of those whose human aspirations have been thwarted on every side and who have been sustained only by hope? Must we declare their hope delusion? … If we feel such questions as these keenly, we must reflect seriously on the possibility of belief in life after death, however reluctant we may be to treat this questionable idea" (Cobb, 1969, pp. 100–101).

Thus it is that on the last page of the chapter on evil and God's power, Cobb describes his ideas about the next life. "Eternal punishment is clearly disproportionate to any human desert, and indeed any idea of retributive punishment, however slight, raises nearly insuperable problems. I can think of God only as offering to each person in each moment of that other life whatever possibility of satisfaction he might attain, just as I see him doing in this life. This does not mean that all would be offered some kind of immediate blessedness there, any more than this is a possibility here. At times the best possible may involve acute pain and suffering, just as in this life ... But it does mean that the image of God's action should be that of the hound of heaven rather than of a moralistic judge" (Cobb, 1969, p. 102).

This description rings true to me. On the topic of justice rendered, I have already endorsed Tillich's idea that God is more interested in creative justice than in either the retributive justice of punishment or the attributive justice of extrinsic rewards. Moreover, I feel that, in the next life, those who find their joy and their meaning in helping others in this life—those who have made compassion second nature—will have the opportunity of further fulfillment, although it may require pain and suffering for love's sake. And God will still seek full reconciliation with the human race, I believe.

Tillich's Conceptualization of the Next Life, and My Conclusions

I understand Cobb's main concerns, in adding this visualization of life after death, to be (1) the need for the value that God preserves from the world's history to have life (subjectivity) of its own, and (2) regarding "the fate of those whose human aspirations have been thwarted" in this life, the need to address the seemingly eternal loss of possibilities of good life *in this world*, especially on behalf of those who have to suffer all their lives. These concerns are both addressed in Tillich's *Systematic Theology*.

In the third volume he described a conception of eternal life that included God's retaining the good that develops in this world, calling it a retention that is not an inert memory but is instead living (Tillich, 1963, pp. 399–400). The subjectivity Cobb seeks is therefore represented, and a new life based on the good of life as lived in this world speaks to Cobb's second concern, since the features of this life that God deems "good" include the possibilities of good yet to be realized. Those possibilities are, in fact, the grounding of the new subjectivity. (Near the end of *The Secret Message of Jesus*, McLaren provides similar imagery, according to which God harvests from this world "the good fruit of all times and places—purged of chaff, winnowed of evil—leaving only pure seeds full of new possibilities for a bright future" (McLaren, 2006, p.260).)

Perhaps there is, in the next life, what we would call a synthesis of Cobb's image of an immanent God who calls (without coercing) with Tillich's imagery of a transcendent God who retains the good, including the possibilities for good, in this life and gives them new life. That possibility seems to me to be a way in which God could exercise creative justice as the guiding principle. Creative justice would operate in two complementary ways. First, in Tillich's imagery, the possibilities for good that are thwarted by bad events are not ultimately gone for good. And second, the possibilities for good that arise out of bad events have their chance to play out as well. This second benefit needs some elaboration.

In real life, much good often arises, ultimately, from bad events. Of course, the reverse is also true, but Tillich's conceptualization does provide a positive reason for God's allowing the bad to happen—namely, to give a chance, after the fact of a bad event, for good to arise from it, good that would otherwise never have a chance to happen, or at least would be unlikely to happen.

We see this all the time, even in this life, as persons are called by God's Spirit within them (whether or not they recognize it as such) to bring good out of tragedy, to make this imperfect world a little better. The abduction of a child leads to a coordinated network providing improved responses to the report of missing children. Funds and foundations begun in memorial to persons whose lives are cut short help to prevent future deaths of those types. Cities savaged by earthquakes are rebuilt with structures better able to handle such disasters thereafter. Had two world wars not happened, much of the good of our world today would never have occurred, for the simple reason that the people doing those good deeds would never have been born, because their parents' lives would have been very different.

Do those sorts of good outcomes outweigh the suffering of the calamities that allowed their existence? Often they do not. Perhaps they never do. But they are in themselves good, and they reflect God's will that we should continue to participate in the building of God's kingdom on earth, *whatever* happens.

The only way I can picture how this might work would be to envision an unending sequence of next worlds, branching out to produce new, different events and eventually new, different people. (For example, all of those "future worlds" in which World War I was averted—thereby giving another chance to the possibilities for good that were aborted by that war—would not include me, for I would never have been born.) I'm reminded here of a passage from Jorge Luis Borges' *The Garden of Forking Paths*, quoted in the preface of a book about the many-worlds interpretation of quantum mechanics. It provides "a picture, incomplete yet not false, [envisioning] a dizzily growing, ever spreading network of diverging, converging and parallel times … We do not exist in most of them. In some you exist and not I, while in others I do, and you do not, and in yet others both of us exist" (Borges, as quoted in DeWitt and Graham, 1973, p. vi).

I should add that that quotation is about as close as the Cobb-Tillich imagery ever gets to the many-worlds interpretation of quantum mechanics as traditionally conceived. The "new world" in one is after the fact, at chosen times, and is accomplished by God's purposeful "reimagining," whereas in the other a splitting occurs at the happening of every event and has no purpose behind it.

Perhaps a down-to-earth analogy would be helpful. I think of a novelist who has carried a group of characters through many preceding novels but is now stuck on a crucial chapter of her next novel. Over and over she rewrites the chapter, starting from various points, trying to reach a certain kind of outcome while at the same time staying true to the personalities she has already established for her characters. Time for her is very different from time for her characters. And just as those characters live in her mind, I believe that in some sense we (albeit privileged as we are to have free will) can be thought of as living in the mind of God, in whom "we live and move and have our being" (Acts: 17:28).

For some, the notion of God restarting the world at a chosen "moment"—in the way that a novelist can pick a point (a fictional time) in the novel and begin revising the story from that point—might seem to be disallowed by relativity theory. Basically, the aspect of time that we can study is, as Einstein once said, what clocks measure. And that aspect has been found to have some very strange properties, including the fact that every physical object is its own clock, whose recorded time (such as the age of a rock) differs ever so slightly from other objects, relative to which it has ever accelerated. It thus would seem as though God's restarting time for the whole world at a particular moment is a meaningless concept. However, one feature of relativity theory is that all observers at a single location in space and time must always agree on the specific features (readings on meter sticks, time readings on clocks, etc.) at that same location and time. The clock readings may be different, but they are unambiguous. If God is omnipresent, all objects (including human beings) exist at the same reading on "God's clock," regardless of what their individual clocks might read.

A final note is in order. Believers in God hope for some sort of spirit-to-spirit encounter with God after they die. Christians, for example, hope to encounter Christ. The Cobb-Tillich imagery does not preclude an after-death experience of the holy, a fuller experience than is possible in this life; it concerns only how a person's life (and the whole world, as well) might be resumed at a point prior to the person's death, a point that is propitious in regard to the overall advancement of God's kingdom on earth. When we die, we might, for example, review, in the full presence of God's Spirit, our individual pasts and the effects of our decisions on others. That would be a sort of "judgment day" with creative justice as its purpose, if it helped to determine the point at which each person's life would be restarted. And it would answer Cobb's concern for the man who willingly dies for the sake of others: his judgment day experience would be a happy one; afterwards his life would restart at some point in "our time" at which the possibilities for good (for him and for the world) outweigh the possibilities of evil and natural calamity.

I doubt seriously that either Cobb or Tillich believed his conceptualization to fully and literally capture God's will in regard to the next life. I certainly don't see the union of their ideas doing that, either. *These are just images, hinting at the unsearchable strength and depth of God's love,* as proclaimed in Jesus' teachings and illustrated both by Jesus' willingness to die for our sakes and by God's willingness to let him do so. It does seem to me that something along the lines of Tillich's and Cobb's ideas may hint at what the next life is like. But in any case, I believe that God loves us—all people everywhere—with a love that will never end, and that is good enough for me.

REFERENCES

Armstrong, K. *Twelve Steps to a Compassionate Life*. New York: A. A. Knopf, 2010.

Barclay, W. *The Daily Study Bible: The Gospel of Matthew, Vol. 2*, second ed. Edinburgh: The Saint Andrew Press, 1958.

Barbour, I. G. *Issues in Science and Religion*. New York: Harper and Row, 1966.

Barbour, I. G. *Religion in an Age of Science*. New York: HarperCollins Publishers, 1990.

Barbour, I. G. *When Science Meets Religion*. New York: HarperCollins Publishers, 2000.

Beck, D. M. *Through the Gospels to Jesus*. New York: Harper & Brothers, 1954.

Bower, B. "Visions for All." *Science News*, April 7, 2012, 22-25, 2012.

Cobb, J. B., Jr. *God and the World*. Philadelphia: Westminster Press, 1969.

deLaubenfels, P. M. (letter to the editor) *Science News*, June 20, 1992, 411, 1992.

deLaubenfels, P. M. (letter to the editor) *Science News*, August 14, 2010, 34, 2010.

DeWitt, B. S. and N. Graham, eds. *The Many-Worlds Interpretation of Quantum Mechanics*. Princeton: Princeton University Press, 1973.

Dostoyevsky, F. *The Brothers Karamazov*. Trans. by A. R. MacAndrew. New York: Bantam Books, 1970.

Durant, W. *The Story of Philosophy*. New York: Pocket Books, 1953.

Ehrman, B. *The Orthodox Corruption of Scripture: The Effect of Early Christological Controversies on the Text of the New Testament.* New York: Oxford University Press, 1993.

Ehrman, B. *Jesus: Apocalyptic Prophet of the First Century*. New York: Oxford University Press, 1999.

Ehrman, B. *The Historical Jesus, Part 2*. Chantilly, Va.: The Teaching Company, 2000.

Ehrman, B. *From Jesus to Constantine: A History of Early Christianity, Part I.* Chantilly, Va.: The Teaching Company, 2004.

Ehrman, B. *Forged: Writing in the Name of God: Why the Bible's Authors Are Not Who We Think They Are.* New York: HarperCollins Publishers, 2011.

Funk, R. W., R. W. Hoover, and the Jesus Seminar. *The Five Gospels: What Did Jesus Really Say?* New York: HarperCollins, 1997. Copyrighted in 2003 by Polebridge Press, Santa Rosa, Calif.

Funk, R. W., and the Jesus Seminar. *The Acts of Jesus: The Search for the Authentic Deeds of Jesus.* New York: HarperCollins Publishers, 1998.

Gomes, P. J. *The Scandalous Gospel of Jesus: What's So Good about the Good News?* New York: HarperCollins Publishers, 2007.

Harris, S. L. *Understanding the Bible*, fifth edition. Mountain View, Calif: Mayfield Publishing Company, 2000.

Heisenberg, W. *Physics and Philosophy: The Revolution in Modern Science. P.S. Insights, Interviews, and More.* New York: HarperCollins Publishers, 1962.

Hordern, W. E. *A Layman's Guide to Protestant Theology*, revised ed. New York: Macmillan Publishing Company, 1968.

Howell, J. "Why Do Bad Things Happen?" *The Charlotte Observer,* May 30, 1994, 13A, 1994.

Jaki, S. L. *The Relevance of Physics.* Chicago: University of Chicago Press, 1966.

Kaegi, W. E., and P. W. White, eds. "Rome: Late Republic and Principate." *University of Chicago Readings in West Civilization*, vol. 2. Chicago: University of Chicago Press, 1986.

Lapide, P. *The Resurrection of Jesus: A Jewish Perspective.* Trans. by W. Linss. Eugene, OR: Wipf and Stock Publishers, 1982. Previously published in 1982 by Augsburg Fortress Publishing House.

Lewis, C. S. *The Great Divorce.* New York: Macmillan, 1946.

Lüdemann, G. *The Resurrection of Christ: A Historical Inquiry.* Amherst, N.Y.: Prometheus Books, 2004.

Luhrmann, T. M. *When God Talks Back: Understanding the American Evangelical Relationship with God.* New York: Alfred A. Knopf, 2012.

McLaren, B. D. *The Secret Message of Jesus: Uncovering the Truth That Could Change Everything.* Nashville: Thomas Nelson, 2006.

McLaren, B. D. *A New Kind of Christianity: Ten Questions That Are Transforming the Faith.* New York: HarperCollins Publishers, 2010.

Meeks, W. A., general editor. *The HarperCollins Study Bible.* New York: HarperCollins, 1993.

Mellowes, M., producer and writer. *From Jesus to Christ: The First Christians* (video series shown on PBS channels, copyrighted 2009 by PBS Distribution). Boston: WGBH Educational Foundation, 1998, 2003.

Mermin, N. D. "What's Bad about This Habit." *Physics Today,* 62 (5), 8-9, 2009.

Pais, A. *Niels Bohr's Times, In Physics, Philosophy, and Polity.* New York: Oxford University Press, 1991.

Peacocke, A. *Paths from Science Towards God: The End of All Our Exploring.* Oxford: Oneworld Publications, 2010.

Perrin, N. *The New Testament: An Introduction.* New York: Harcourt Brace Jovanovich, 1974.

Perrin, N., K. C. Hansen, ed. *Parable and Gospel.* Minneapolis: Augsburg Fortress, 2003.

Rees, M. *Just Six Numbers: The Deep Forces That Shape the Universe.* New York: BasicBooks, 2000.

Rhoads, D., J. Dewey, and D. Michie. *Mark as Story: An Introduction to the Narrative of a Gospel.* Minneapolis: Fortress Press, 1999.

Rigden, J. S. *Einstein 1905: The Standard of Greatness.* Cambridge, Mass.: Harvard University Press, 2005.

Ruark, H. G. *Blessed Are You….* Laurinburg, N.C.: The Bill Evans Press, 1960.

Russell, R. J. *Cosmology from Alpha to Omega: The creative mutual interaction of theology and science.* Minneapolis: Augsburg Fortress, 2008.

Stapp, H. P. "The Copenhagen Interpretation." *The American Journal of Physics,* 40 (8), 1098–1116, 1972.

Tillich, P. *Love, Power and Justice: Ontological Analyses and Ethical Applications.* New York: Oxford University Press, 1960.

Tillich, P. *Systematic Theology, Vol. III.* Chicago: University of Chicago Press, 1963.

Walborn, S. P., M. de O. Terra Cunha, S. J. Nascimento de Pádua, and C. H. Monken. "Quantum Erasure." *American Scientist,* 91 (4), 336–343, 2003.

Wilcox, D. J. *In Search of God and Self: Renaissance and Reformation Thought.* Boston: Houghton Mifflin,

1975. Reissued in 1987 by Waveland Press, Prospect Heights, Ill.

Will, G. "What We Owe to What We Eat." *Newsweek*, July 18, 2005, 66, 2005.

Woodward, K. L. "Rethinking the Resurrection." *Newsweek*, April 8, 1996, 60-70, 1996.

Printed in the USA
CPSIA information can be obtained
at www.ICGtesting.com
LVHW011153180624
783442LV00010B/60

9 798890 914170